EXPERIENCING
God
WITH YOUR
CHILDREN

EXPERIENCING *God*

WITH YOUR CHILDREN

KATHY COFFEY

A Crossroad Book
The Crossroad Publishing Company
New York

1997

The Crossroad Publishing Company
370 Lexington Avenue, New York, NY 10017

Printed in the United States of America

Library of Congress Cataloging-in-Publication Data

Coffey, Kathy.
    Experiencing God with your children / Kathy Coffey ; foreword by
Dolores Curran.
        p.   cm.
    ISBN 0-8245-1647-8 (pbk.)
    1. Family – Religious life. 2. Coffey, Kathy. 3. Catholic Church –
Membership.   I. Title.
BX2351.C54   1997
248.4–dc21   96-36912
                                                                  CIP

For my sons, David and Sean,
who have taught me more about God
than any course in theology

CONTENTS

PART III
GUIDING THE QUEST

FOREWORD

by Dolores Curran

THIS SUPERB WORK on family spirituality makes me want to burn my own. Now that I've confessed to the sin of covetousness, I feel free to share my reflections on this extraordinary book. *Experiencing God with Your Children* is neither a guidebook on Christian parenting nor a collection of family religious rituals, so readers looking for a rundown on the habits of highly effective Christian parents or hints on rearing children eager to pray the nightly rosary will have to search in other books. But there are plenty of those already out there, including my own.

I label Kathy Coffey's book extraordinary because it is a readable and relatable *theology of family spirituality from the lived experience*. As such it deserves a place in both the theology and family sections of libraries and bibliographies. It also demands to be read by theologians, who tend to avoid both family and the lived experience as worthy of academic study or spiritual reflection and downright shun them when paired. Nonparent church folk will, naturally, find this work valuable in understanding families in their parishes and the world but they will also gain insight into who they are as a result of their own family life — a frequently neglected area of reflection for many. They are who they are because of their families, warts and halos. We all are, but parents have the advantage of learning more about ourselves as we witness the development of our children.

Parents will embrace and absorb this book because it is the most convincing one around on the spirituality of what we are already doing. We've been told this over and over again, but we don't really believe it. The author, using daily experiences like dental visits and first drivers, presents profound insights into the spirituality of the moments of family life, a lived spirituality too often unsuspected by parents and children.

She states her two themes up front: launching an exploration and coming home, but she fleshes these themes out in language that touches the soul. "While launching into God may carry some noble overtones of a heroic odyssey, it is also, paradoxically, like coming home. The link between home and a person shouldn't surprise children. They know the difference the minute they walk through the door after school. If the parent is home, there is sometimes a smell of cooking, a trace of perfume or shaving lotion, the sound of a radio or television, a drill or a typewriter, a 'How was your day?' filtering through the commotion.

"When the parent isn't home, the absence is obvious. No one has turned up the heat, collected the mail, or fed the dog. The rooms are silent; on the kitchen table cereal congeals in the breakfast bowls. 'Home alone' can powerfully symbolize the absence of God."

It is not surprising the author is an award-winning poet. Her poetry shines through her prose in a way that uplifts and celebrates the ordinariness of family life. But she is also prophet and practitioner. If, as one definition goes, a prophet is one who reveals God to others and others to God, she belongs on the list of modern-day prophets. I guess this is the most remarkable part of the book to me — she constantly reveals the presence and reality of God in the midst of humdrum repetitive life in the laundry room and does it in such a way that I believe her. As to being practitioner, she's been there (in fact, she's still there) and readers will find themselves in the "why do we hafta go to church" serial, the clutter syndrome, and the motel room on family vacation.

After reading her manuscript, I was almost sorry my children have grown and left the nest. I let too many sacred moments flee by unnoticed because I was enamored of calendars and clocks. I was efficient. I was chasing perfection. I was foolish.

Somehow, our children survived, launched their exploration into adulthood, and, to our great joy, even return home occasionally, unbidden and happy to be here. Our experience as parents is fleshed out in the closing paragraph of an early chapter:

"Children who are securely grounded have the confidence to venture forth because they know the way home. From their love for each other, parents and children can learn much about God. That home is the starting point and the end of our theology should not seem so odd. For Jesus, the great adventure began in the small circle of affection at Bethlehem, and ended in the circle of his mother's arms."

So well written. I covet. Mea culpa...

ACKNOWLEDGMENTS

PATRICE TUOHY, managing editor of *U.S. Catholic*, suggested the first in a series of three articles that became the basis for this book. "Eight Things I'd Like to Teach My Kids about God" then received the Religious Public Relations Council's Award of Excellence, and led to two more articles in the series.

Some of this material appeared originally in *America, Momentum, Praying, Spiritual Life, Abbey Press PrayerNotes, St. Anthony Messenger, Catholic Digest, Eucharistic Minister, Parish Family Digest, The Family,* and *Celebration.*

Acknowledgment is gratefully given for permission to reprint as follows:

Page 25: From *A Sleep of Prisoners* by Christopher Fry. Reprinted by permission of Oxford University Press.

Page 36: From "(untitled)" from *The Night Train and the Golden Bird,* by Peter Meinke, © 1977. Reprinted by permission of the University of Pittsburgh Press.

Page 96: Excerpts from *J. B.: A Play in Verse* by Archibald MacLeish. Copyright © 1956, 1957, 1958 by Archibald MacLeish. Reprinted by permission of Houghton Mifflin Co. All rights reserved.

Page 100: From "The Work of Happiness" from *Collected Poems 1930–1933* by May Sarton. Copyright © 1993, 1988, 1984, 1980, 1974 by May Sarton. Reprinted by permission of W. W. Norton & Company, Inc.

Page 114: From "Poem in Prose" by Archibald MacLeish, in Oscar Williams and Edwin Honig, eds., *The Mentor Book of Major American Poets.* Used by permission of Random House.

Page 124: From *Orphaned Wisdom: Meditations for Lent* by Michael Moynahan, © 1990. Reprinted by permission of Paulist Press.

Page 128: From *Sadako and the Thousand Paper Cranes* by Eleanor Coerr. Reprinted by permission of the Putnam Publishing Group.

INTRODUCTION

S OMETIMES THE YOUNGEST of our four children gets special attention. Katie and I have some of our best discussions as we hunch over cocoa (hers) and coffee (mine) in the earliest glimmers of morning. "What's your favorite drink?" she asks. I'm surprised to discover there's no simple, clear-cut answer; it depends on the season and the time of day.

"Nothing better than hot chocolate after skiing. But then, a hot July afternoon calls for a frosty root beer. Apple cider at Halloween; eggnog at Christmas. Big gulps of water after a run or a hike. A Chablis to sip on a picnic beneath leaves turning gold, a robust burgundy to wash down a spaghetti dinner with friends, and a soft rosé in candlelight." The list could go on, probably exhausting Katie's initial flicker of interest. Because Katie's mom has an odd twist of mind, the variety of drinks turned to thoughts theological. Our conversation helped me see that the cup of water Christ asks us to give each other in his name could be a steamy bowl of soup in winter, a Popsicle in summer.

How providential that God should also have infinite variety! For all the different seasons in children's growing up, a different face of God can turn to their deepest longings and respond to their deepest desires. Not that we fashion God into silly putty, shaped only to the urge of the moment. But our Scripture and tradition are rich with revelations of God that keep us constantly entranced and in love. My favorite phrase in "Amazing Grace" is, "When we've been there ten thousand years, bright shining as the sun, we've no less days to sing God's praise than when we first begun." We can explore the nature of God throughout a lifetime and never reach the end.

To put this exploration of God into terms that Katie might understand, I compare it to launching a frail craft into a vast ocean: something about the adventure is overwhelming; yet something else about it is enticing. The ocean is a colossal force, a presence huge beyond our imagining. Yet at the same time, the tiniest creatures make a home there; on its shores we find shells smaller than an infant's toenail.

While launching into God may carry some noble overtones of a heroic odyssey, it is also, paradoxically, like coming home. The link between home and a person shouldn't surprise children. They know

13

the difference the minute they walk through the door after school. If the parent is home, there is sometimes a smell of cooking, a trace of perfume or shaving lotion, the sound of a radio or television, a drill or a typewriter, a "How was your day?" filtering through the commotion.

When the parent isn't home, the absence is obvious. No one has turned up the heat, collected the mail, or fed the dog. The rooms are silent; on the kitchen table cereal congeals in the breakfast bowls. "Home alone" can powerfully symbolize the absence of God.

On the other hand, our first, most precious learnings about God can come only at home. If, in that small sphere, we do not fall in love with God, it would be pointless to continue our quest. Why would we want to know more? Of course, grace can make surprising reversals; people who have grown up with punitive images of a hostile God have been able to change those images. But if we would give our children the best introduction to the divine person, we will begin our exploration informally, poking into the nooks and crannies of home, where God is a dear and familiar presence.

Parents and children who do meet God at home are more inclined to broaden their orbit and find God everywhere. Our family can turn a hotel into home in seconds; the pristine room fills with our baggage and paraphernalia faster than I would like. One son has a habit of dumping everything from his suitcase into one corner, as if to stake out his territory and make this foreign land familiar ground. Perhaps the same instinct moves mountain climbers to hang their colors on peaks or astronauts to plant the American flag in the dust of the moon.

The gesture is fitting since it combines the two themes of this book: launching an exploration and coming home. Children who are securely grounded have the confidence to venture forth because they know the way home. From what is close and dear, parents and children can learn much about God who is infinite and powerful. Using home as the starting point and the end of our theology should not seem so odd. For Jesus, earthly life began in the small circle of affection at Bethlehem, and ended in the circle of his mother's arms.

PART I

Stars to Steer By

Sailors who do celestial navigation take their bearings by several stars. To find out where they are and calculate where they want to go, they measure lines of sight against the horizon with sextants and charts. So we who launch an exploration into God look to similar guiding lights. We characterize the quest as both exploration and homecoming, because elements of both are essential. We rely on the wisdom, innocence, and energy of our children, finding richer meaning because our voyage is connected to theirs. God draws us through the beauty of creation and transforms us through our love for each other. Guided by such stars, the voyage is an adventure worth launching.

— *1* —

LAUNCHING

W HEN OUR FAMILY OF SIX visits the coast, we never need to plan our first activity. Everyone knows the unchanging routine: land at the airport, rent the car, drive to the nearest beach, plunge into the ocean. In the car, we exchange winter clothes for swimsuits, shed the shoes, and apply the sunscreen. No one ever questions the established ritual; no one ever deviates. No one has ever mentioned stopping for a snack; anyone who tried would be trounced at the very suggestion.

First, we smell the salt air. Then we run pell-mell, leaping and shouting giddily, down to the shore. Nothing can prevent us from jumping into the foaming surf: some driving force compels us to the sea. When they are small, the children run hand-in-hand with older siblings or parents, but they are quickly caught up in the dizzying joy of the race, and soon outrun their elders. With waves crashing and kids cavorting, it is a serendipitous scene.

Perhaps it is like that when parents and children enter into a joint exploration of God. How can we *not* go? No matter what other agendas concern us, no matter what wisdom we want to give our children, the divine person is uniquely compelling, drawing us with an infinite love. The search for God becomes a quest for creator, lover, parent, friend, our reason for being, the meaning of our lives, the beauty, the fulfillment of our days. A life that lacks this center seems an unimaginable desert, a barren land without water. Following our natural pull toward God is colossally important; nothing else matters more.

Comparing God to the ocean is not new. When St. Augustine tells God in his *Confessions,* "I was swept up to Thee by Thy beauty,"[1] we can easily imagine the reflection of a full moon or an apricot sunset trailing over the waters. For the thirteenth-century German mystic Mechthild of Magdeburg, "the essential quality of God's grace is fluidity." She sees the Trinity not as an abstraction, but as an inexhaustible, fecund, flowing "torrent of love." The ebb and flow of this "rippling tide...flows secretly from God into the soul and draws it mightily back into its Source."[2]

16

In our own day, Bill Wilson, the cofounder of Alcoholics Anonymous, cried to God for help with his chronic alcoholism. In response he felt a presence which "seemed like a veritable sea of living spirit."[3]

A watery metaphor for God not only has a long history, but it has been easily accessible for us and our children. They know what it is to stand beside the ocean: vast, powerful, thundering fiercely, teeming with life in its unfathomable depths. Yet at the same time, its foam curls kindly around our toes. We lie on its warm shore, lulled by the soothing rhythm of its waves. Children play in the soft sand; teenagers set up volleyball nets within reach of the spray; adults are drawn to something larger than they are, big enough to challenge, close enough to embrace. After a day at the shore, we may be exhausted, but at some deep level, we are also refreshed. We have met a force that is large and elemental, yet at the same time tied to the salt in our tears, the chemicals in our bloodstreams.

Just as the sea exerts its pull, so the mystery of God draws us in and on. We enter that presence because we can never exhaust it, yet every chord of our being tingles in recognition. For this person, we were created. Vast and small, untouchable yet personal, this God evokes our deepest capacity for wonder. When we finally do meet God, it won't be a surprise, but a face made familiar by our longing and our search.

For some people to plunge into God, they must jettison, like cumbersome cargo, their negative, punitive images of God. They may have learned in childhood that God was the fierce wielder of the battle ax, the frowning keeper of the books. It is understandable why they would not want to poke a toe into the sea of God or lift an oar in what poet Anne Sexton calls this "awful rowing toward God." Mention the divine name and they run fearfully in the opposite direction.

While some may think this terror is the product of past rigidities in narrow, archaic schooling systems, the "God as threat" theory persists. Recently a mother tried to quiet her son in church as he pursued normal two-year-old activities. His racing plastic cars down the pews, with a soft accompanying narrative, was not particularly annoying to anyone else, but the mother became increasingly vexed. Finally, she thwacked the child in fury and hissed, "Stop it, Sherman! You're in God's house!" A sure-fire guarantee that Sherman would never want to revisit such a stifling residence of such an unwelcoming host.

The research of Father Andrew Greeley seems especially relevant to the kind of God-images people develop. In his book *Religion as*

Poetry he designed a "Grace Scale" to measure a respondent's image of God — as mother versus father, lover versus judge, spouse versus master, and friend versus king. He discovered that those who chose the first term in each pair have a more positive, hope-filled attitude toward life, seeing it as gift rather than trial or burden. Now the challenge: parents' profound influence can bring children to a high grace scale. While Greeley has not researched children's effect on parents, one suspects the effect might be similar. When we are alert to the divine presence in each other, we can tap an underlying current bringing us another dimension of beauty, meaning, and power.

I remember as a child the momentous occasion when we would visit Lake Michigan. The official destination was of course Chicago, but to me the city was simply an appendage attached to that awesome body of water. My mother would make sure I visited museums and shopped at Marshall Field's, but I thought the attraction of the lake outshone anything else Chicago could offer. Given a choice, I'd make a beeline for its shores.

That memory stirs over thirty years later when I take my own children to a city near water. Given multiple options of zoos, shopping malls, museums, playgrounds or space centers, they inevitably choose a day at the shore. What's the attraction?

Part of it must be the mystery. This vast presence does not say a word; it does not burden us with talk or trivia. It moves, simply and grandly, millions of droplets in the light. It connects us to another dimension, a broader framework for our lives. Surely the horizon where sky and water blend symbolizes the infinite for which we long. As small children or as adults who feel sorely our limitations, we want to be part of something larger, more complete than we are.

As a child, I enjoyed wrapping my tongue and my mind around a doxology impossible to understand, but nonetheless intriguing: "as it was in the beginning, is now, and ever shall be, world without end. Amen." In contrast to the city on the shore which changes hourly, the lake or the sea seems immutable. Infinite and unchanging, it is naturally linked with the presence of God. We pray over the waters that will be used for baptism at the Easter Vigil: "At the very dawn of creation your Spirit breathed on the waters, making them the wellspring of all holiness." The waters of Genesis, the Red Sea, the Jordan have always held symbolic value for humankind; perhaps we see in their depths the God who was and is and always will be.

Now during most of the year, our family lives in landlocked Colorado, with the Rocky Mountains our touchstone to creation's magnificence. I had thought perhaps the novelty of the ocean explained its attraction. But I was delighted to discover that it holds the same sway over those who live in close proximity to its tides — all the time.

In one sequence of the IMAX film *The Living Seas,* a Palau islander, who lives in the Pacific east of the Philippines, pilots a speedboat across the sea. Over the roar of the boat motor, he explains his family's constantly growing relationship with their ocean environment: "It's a kind of courtship."

His words are illustrated by the actions that follow. He and his two children, wearing scuba diving equipment, somersault backward off their boat into the shining waters. "I want them to love the sea," the father's voice-over continues as they swim through a coral reef. "I don't care if they like fast boats; the important thing is that they learn to reverence the sea."

The children feed the schools of tropical fish surrounding them in an explosion of color. On the scales of fish, hot pinks, paisley prints, neon stripes, and polka dots swish gracefully, as if a fabric store had unrolled all its bolts in one stunning display.

The father explains that reverence for the sea is a long tradition in his culture. Each island family tends a section of the reef as they would a garden. Captivated by the aesthetics, the fluttering motion, the colors, we wonder, "How could the children *not* follow such a tradition?"

Perhaps it is like that as we invite children to another kind of courtship: exploring God. Together we plunge off the safe shores into the mystery, never knowing what we'll find, but sure that adventure awaits. God rewards our quest, being at once the vast sea, the boat, the diver and the shore, the end of the voyage and its beginning. In seeking God, we may also find our best selves, the part of us that, child-like, plays trustfully near the roaring waves.

As we launch our exploration, we may feel frightened or unsure, but our children deserve whatever risks we take. History is full of examples of people doing things they never dreamed they could — for the sake of their children. In gentle, unspoken ways, our children count on us to give them the best we know. How could we squander their confidence and our own precious talents on a less worthy quest? How could we waste time watching the shallow trickle of a drainage ditch if the Pacific pounded across the street?

The quest described here has definite parameters. I write as a mother of two sons and two daughters ages eleven to twenty-two, drawing on memories of them all at different ages. While I have enormous empathy for fathers, my husband of twenty-five years is the expert in that department. I am grateful for those who have researched and written on the fatherly role, but he lives that commitment daily. After teaching fifth graders, he comes home to our children, a fathering feat in itself. He constantly reminds me of our rich blessings: our children, health, education, work, and travel are gifts from God's hands which we could never appreciate enough. Despite God's gracious gifts, we are by no stretch of the imagination the perfect family. We sulk and fume, bicker and squabble as much as anyone else. Knowing our limitations, I have asked many friends for their stories as well, and appreciate the way these have broadened my frame of reference.

Although I admire the parents of physically or mentally challenged children, I have little experience there. I have been particularly grateful to the parents who do know this realm and whose freely shared stories give some glimmer of their joys and struggles. While the language used to describe our quest may be more familiar to people of liturgical traditions, spirituality has broad horizons; the voyage into God is open to anyone.

For those who still hesitate to launch into God, it may be consoling to know that our children are our best, most reassuring companions on the voyage. Unburdened by the baggage of preconceived notions or clear demarcations between "holy" and "ordinary," they gladly join in the excitement. Like the child in Scripture, they offer what they have, even if it's only five barley loaves and two fishes. Surely Jesus, who sailed the sea of Galilee, called fisherfolk to follow him, and transformed that child's little lunch, will bless our efforts, too. His partnership in our efforts can make a miracle.

— 2 —

EXPLORING

IT MAY SURPRISE some people to view the shared activity described here in terms of exploration. Are we not, after all, handing down to our children a faith heritage centuries old? Haven't the finest human minds already worked out the answers to our questions about God, ourselves, and our relationships? What could be left to discover? What frontier could we possibly explore? Surely it is presumptuous to describe this activity like the adventures of Lewis, Clark, and Sacajawea?

Indeed, we can assume our rightful places among the great explorers. We call this activity "exploring" because it's an accurate term for many twentieth-century folks who have abandoned the old certitudes and pat answers. Just as our faith looks different from our parents', so our children's will probably evolve differently from ours.

In terms of inviting our children to join us, "exploring" sounds like fun. The word has an appeal that words like "school," "religious studies," "tests," and "textbooks" will never capture. The adventure of entering the unknown intrigues most children, and any adults who have not completely calcified. On a natural plane, hiking a new trail, trying a foreign food, or entering a city we've not yet visited lures us: we never know what treasure we might find. Around the next corner, we may discover a lovely vista, a hidden lake, a food, a place, an author, or a friend who will become a lifelong favorite. That's why we press beyond the next bend in the road, past the familiar, into the unknown. When the unexplored frontier is no longer there to tantalize, our lives are somehow diminished.

If we frame the parent's task as merely doling out answers, we have misunderstood and demeaned our role. That narrow definition also restricts our children to talking heads, or computers programmed to process knowledge. We who live with children know that they are far more complex. The whole child is an amazing combination of feelings, senses, imagination, body, and intellect. To reduce that complexity to an information bank is to insult the God who created them. "How wondrous and manifold are your works," sang the psalmist. Only in that spirit can we fully appreciate the gifts that our children are.

In "The Soulful Educator," a talk to the 1994 Los Angeles Religious Education Congress, Thomas Moore, author of *The Care of the Soul,* proposed that metaphors of clocks and computers are too shallow to describe human beings. People in medieval times used instead the image of the night sky: infinite, awesome, and mysterious. If this metaphor fits young people whom a teacher meets professionally for a short time each week, how much truer it is for children with whom we live twenty-four hours a day for some twenty years!

A cognitive or "heady" approach to God restricts children to one response: here's the information. Learn it. As a survivor of Baltimore Catechism religious education (memorize it or die of embarrassment), I can attest to the lack of ownership in that approach. It provides ready answers to questions we haven't asked; it obscures any connection between faith themes and our lived experience. To give children rigidly formulated doctrine does not invite them into mystery or bring into play their gifts of wonder and imagination. Such a narrow stance recalls the eighteenth-century Hebrew story of the blacksmith.

Rabbi Abraham Heschel tells of a young man who became an apprentice and soon learned all the tricks of the trade. He knew how to hold the tongs, use the bellows, hit the anvil. When he finished his apprenticeship, he found a job in the palace smithy. But all his skill with the tools turned out to be useless. He had never learned how to kindle a spark.

The parent's role in kindling the spark of faith in their children is unique, quite distinct from the professional teacher's. In the Indian tradition, a guru is worth a hundred teachers, a father is worth a hundred gurus, and a mother is worth a hundred fathers. While we can reinforce at home whatever formal religious instruction our children receive, we also have an intimate relationship with our children that no professional can approach. If we are fortunate enough to share the child's whole affective domain, we would be crazy to relegate ourselves to the box of textbook learning. We are likely to be around when children have their most profound experiences, which bring them closest to God. As most teachers would agree, those don't usually come in a classroom.

Parents also have a unique, limited time frame. Most of us don't want to waste the eighteen or twenty years we have with our children on information they can easily pick up elsewhere. I admire the awesome intellectual structures of theology and will encourage my children to study these when they are older. But I also know that they won't give a hoot about theology if they haven't fallen in love with the person it's all about.

No guy falls in love with a girl's femur. No girl loves a man because he's so productive. A long, caring relationship is not a question of memorizing the chemicals in the beloved's bloodstream. When we begin a friendship, we don't usually file information about the person. We discover a wicked sense of humor or we find a lot in common. If exploration is the best part of launching a human relationship, it may also be true of a relationship with the divine.

The very nature of God is mysterious, seducing us beyond the comfort zones. Yet paradoxically, God is a superb linguist, fluent in a multiplicity of ways to communicate. The U.N. simultaneous translation system pales by comparison because it is a vehicle simply for words. When we launch into God with our children, we come across an astonishing variety of communications, and we probably only scratch the surface. For instance, I remember after a week that had been notably horrible, full of frustrations and disappointments, how I sat for almost an hour beneath an apple tree in blossom. Its pure beauty was healing, as people find the warm relaxation of sun on the skin, the many moods in music, the rhythm of waves, or the fragrance of lilacs. These languages require no vocabulary lists, audio tapes, or pronunciation guides. The smallest child can understand their blessing of peace.

Children are also our best guides because their senses, fresh and alive, tingle alertly to stimuli. Their touch has not been petrified; their sight has not yet dimmed; their hearing has not been jaded by overstimulation. They are ripe for a conversation with creation. When God became Word — fleshy and full — God longed to communicate. God did not send the word that oppresses or diminishes or mocks anyone, but the Word that invites us to the fullness of life, that draws us into all the richness the creator intended for us.

Sometimes it comes as a surprise when our children speak the words of comfort or encouragement. My son once consoled me when I agonized that our family never seemed to arrive anywhere on time, organized as precisely or dressed as neatly as other families. He reminded me of the day he'd driven to an important meeting and forgotten the directions for finding the office. He telephoned. I retrieved the vital paper (thoughtfully placed beside the front door, and *left* there) and read it to him over the phone. Then I lamented, "We've got to get it together!"

He soothed, "But our recovery system is so good...."

Perhaps he'd hit on what it means to be redeemed. We can be lazy, self-centered, uncaring clods at times. And yet, the ancients termed that sorry state the *felix culpa,* or happy fault, because it brought us such a redeemer. Salvation history takes on new meaning when condensed into one minor episode of family life.

"All very well," some may harrumph. "But let's not pretend adults don't know more than kids. We can't disguise the years of learning and experience that distinguish us from them."

True — to an extent. But how many of us really understand the mysteries of human life: Why have we been as blessed as we are? Why have we undergone losses we can never explain? Why are the most important things in life — our safety, our health, and the well-being of those we love — ultimately beyond our control? We who consider ourselves older and more knowledgeable have all been paralyzed by a child's innocent question. Just a few of the trickier ones: "Why did Grandma have to die?" "If God is good, why are people starving?" "Why can't I make any friends?" or "Mom, why do you look so sad?"

Anyone who would rush in with pat answers to such dilemmas is either arrogant or stupid. The most sensitive parents might respond: "Here's what I think, but I may be wrong. What do you think?" Or we admit, "That one has puzzled me for a long time. I still haven't figured it out completely, but one day something happened that helped me understand..." and we spin a story. Or we muse, "I once asked my dad that question, and I'll always remember what he said...."

A friend who is completing his doctorate in theology tells how he agonized over a talk he would give at church on some point about God that was elusive. When his three-year-old daughter asked what was troubling him, he explained as best he could that he'd thought hard about God but still wasn't fully understanding God. She reassured him with a touch on his shirt, "Don't worry, Dad. God is right there in your pocket." All our struggles to nuance and refine can sputter into silence before a child's clarity.

The exploratory stance fits the style of Jesus, who invited his friends along on an amazing adventure: come with me, and you will catch people. He didn't seem too intent on dishing out answers, leaving the certainties to the scribes and Pharisees. Instead he told stories with one-line, zinger endings. He asked questions. He invited people along on his journey: "Come and see."

The gospels are filled more with motion than with sitting around in safe places. Jesus could not promise his followers physical shelter: "the Son of Man has nowhere to lay his head" (Luke 9:58). Scripture scholar Eugene La Verdiere points out that even before his adulthood, Jesus' story is filled with travel: Mary's visit with Elizabeth, the journey to Bethlehem, the presentation at the temple.[4] As Jesus' mission unfolds, it is set in the context of a journey to Jerusalem. Chapter beginnings often sound like a travelogue: Gennesaret, Bethsaida, Tyre, Sidon, Capernaum, Jericho, Bethany, criss-crossing the Sea of Galilee.

Not only did Jesus ask his followers to travel physically; he also invited them beyond safe mental nooks and cozy sureties. The people Jesus frequently criticized were the ones with all the answers. The people he liked were the ones who couldn't seem to get it together, who rarely understood what he was talking about, who were simply willing to come along for the ride. Or the voyage. One of Peter's breakthroughs in a series of recognitions came not in the temple, but alone on the high seas in a storm.

In *The Art of Theological Reflection*, authors Patricia Killen and John De Beer write that "exploration is a gift, a trust that God is with us and for us, even when we cannot see how."[5]

Exploration keeps the windows open and the sights fresh. It rules out nothing, takes no refuge in preconceptions. It puts us all on equal footing: the three-year-old is as much of an expert as the sixty-year-old, and both can learn from each other.

Anyone who has hoisted a sail or climbed a mountain with a companion knows the satisfaction of grinning at each other when the harbor is sighted or the heights are achieved. "Cheers!" we say as we exchange a high five. From that time forward, we stand in a special relationship with one another because we have shared the quest. If that is true on a natural plane, how much more it means when, for parents and children

> The enterprise
> Is exploration into God.[6]

— 3 —

HOMECOMING

HOME MUST BE one of those treasures, like health, that we never appreciate until we must do without it. When we're there, it's chaotic: always too much to do in too little time. For moms, home represents a constant series of demands: find this, cook that, answer *me!* Pay attention to *me!* No wonder we seize any chance for a change. No wonder it's exhilarating and stimulating to get away. One of the most frequently cited reasons why people go on vacation is to escape their own clutter.

But if venturing outward is exciting, then so is the opposite movement: homecoming is dear to us, an arrival in which the soul takes deep pleasure. People who travel regularly praise the particular quality of the light, the special horizon that marks home. Much as we relish the outbound voyage, we also love that narrow pencil line, the shore.

On the road, restaurant meals initially seem delicious and glamorous. Then we start longing for a cup of coffee we can make ourselves. We want to pad to the kitchen, barely awake, and be able to reach with squinting eyelids for the pot, finding it on pure instinct. We want to know what's blooming in the garden, what's playing at the local movie, and what gossip is circulating the neighborhood.

Most of all, we want the bodies of our children around us, a swirling that may not entail deep conversation, but the simple flow of daily chatter. We want the brush of their kiss in the morning, the reassurance of the whole family in their own rumpled beds at night. We want the contours of our lives to conform to theirs. A business executive once explained why he'd made elaborate travel arrangements simply to include a quick stop at home during a long trip: "I wanted to hold my children." It must be deeply rooted instinct to fit one's body to another's body, snug as a spoon.

Maria Harris points out in *Proclaim Jubilee!* that the quest or going forth metaphors are essentially masculinized images that need to be complemented by images that arise from women's experience.[7] Women know home as the place of purposeful and productive work, where loneliness is relieved and we learn care. "Home is generally the place for lovemaking and even more, for people-making, a task that often takes eighteen years, and usually, much longer."[8] Hence, we come home not only to our relatives and friends, but to ourselves.

Home is the unrecognized poor relation often passed over when people name the sacred spaces in their lives. While they may list churches, retreat centers, or mountain tops, they neglect the places where they spend most of their time. If God is intent on coming to us, wouldn't it be logical to look for us at home?

Psalm 84:3 gives us a startling image for God who is right at home with us:

> Finally the sparrow has found its home,
> the swallow a nest for its young —
> your altars, Yahweh Sabaoth, O my God.

Yes, God may be terrifying, majestic, awesome, totally beyond our comprehension. But God is also as close as the nesting, slurping, crowding, poking, scrambling, burrowing, cheeping, wormy, sloppy stuff of our days. The marble altar is not too high nor too distant for a messy, twiggy swallow's nest.

God is present in the household because that's where we also find our pure and beautiful drive to nurture and shelter our young. When Jesus welcomed the children, he was surely aware of their sweaty skin, scraped knees, and rowdy shouts. It didn't seem to bother him. He didn't burden the kids with ultimatums or inquire about the legality of their parents' marriages before he touched them. None of this nonsense about "go clean up first, then I'll give you a hug." When we come to God, it's okay to come as we are.

Surely we learn things about God at home that we can learn nowhere else. Whenever I try to describe God's goodness, I remember a poster my daughter made at Sunday school when she was six, colorfully proclaiming, "God is goo."

"What?" I asked, puzzled.

"Teacher called time," she replied.

To move beyond the platitude and own the belief, parents and children must not only pay lip service to God's goodness, but also seek it in each day. Julian of Norwich wrote, "The fullness of joy is to behold God in everything." Even small children can claim that joy: in dandelions and freckles, bear hugs and hot baths, warm bread and comfy sweatshirts. Children's five senses tingle with sensitivity. If after a tough day, the pizza drips fragrantly with mozzarella, the bedtime story delights, and the flannel sheets are warm, they find themselves embraced by God. Jaded people take these pleasures for granted. Saintly folks welcome them as coming from God's hand, brushed by the touch of the beloved.

When we are aware of the ways grace abounds, we live in gratitude, true to all we've been given. It is in the nature of a good God to give abundant gifts, and among the most important are surely the gifts we are to each other. If ever we wonder how God regards us, we need look no further than the parent so riveted to a newborn's face that he or she cannot look away. Holding an infant, many parents feel both wonder and vulnerability.

As one mom said, "At that moment, I knew without a doubt that God existed." But we are also painfully aware that we have given hostages to fortune. The frailty of the human condition becomes achingly apparent as we support a small, wobbly head.

The first gift is followed by many more: the first chuckle, the first step, the first bedtime story, the first corsage. Along with the graces come the challenges: discipline, different values, struggles with authority. Yet even as we bumble through the crises, we thank God. Despite their flaws, our children *live* — our own curious immortality. As we and our children give each other life, we act in the image of God the creator, Jesus, the nurturer and the energizing Spirit.

Furthermore, home is the best place to learn about family resemblance. From millions of possibilities, God created each parent and child with a unique blend of hair color, talents, and personality. On each of us, God marked indelible family similarities, then made us members of a larger family. Just as auburn hair or a prominent nose runs in the family, so each child bears the signs of divine origin and claims Jesus as oldest brother. At home we learn the family ties which translate to a global circle and to a spiritual sphere.

Cherishing each child, God also designed some special task that only he or she can accomplish. No parent can tell a son or daughter exactly what it is, nor should a child feel burdened by it. Instead, an individual calling can give a person a sense of being precious and important, no matter what he or she achieves.

Even young children feel pressure to succeed; parents fret whether preschool will adequately prepare them for Harvard. Being chosen by God means that our personal successes or failures aren't the important thing. It's far more significant to be a partner of Christ and a channel for God's creativity. If we're geared only to the human scale measuring mistakes and achievements, we can easily get ulcers. God's exquisite balance honors the paraplegic as much as the Olympic athlete.

It's impressive to see the quiet fidelity of people who'd never make an official "great" list, but who tend this garden, anchor this family, program this computer, or tune this engine. People who co-create with God bring meaning and reverence to whatever arena is theirs. It's a fascinating idea that the real architects of world peace might be old people sitting in wheelchairs, seeming to stare into space. Whatever outlets our children choose, regardless of their degree of success, it has vitality allied with God's creative force.

Perhaps that's because God is within us. People may need to grow into this understanding, but Thomas Merton's idea of the "point of pure truth," a jewel-like spark which is God's glory within, can bring immense peace. Even fervent believers still grieve, still go ballistic over trivia, still squander energy worrying. But when I center myself, I remember that no matter what happens, God is loving me more than I love myself, wanting only good for me. Even when I am too blind to recognize the "yes" contained within an apparent "no," or the "hello" hidden in "goodbye," God is within, easily accessible, longing to communicate. Regularly taking quiet time for this prayerful conversation is one of the most important things parents can teach children.

Holding this belief can also free children from silly denominational disputes. Jesus settled that question once and for all when he told the Samaritan woman that God lodged neither in Jerusalem nor Samaria, but secure in the human heart.

That points us to a similar belief: that God also lives within others. The incarnate God can wear distressing disguises: as class bully, incompetent teacher, or arrogant cleric. Yet if God is in me, God is also in everyone else. That presence is the basis for respecting every form of human life. It made Jesus quite fond of people no one else would notice. On one hand, his ideal challenges us; on the other, it buoys us to recognize God in the fabric of human love.

In *Les Miserables,* Jean Valjean said: "To love another person is to see the face of God." The loving relationships that fill parents' and children's lives ground them in God. Martin Luther King Jr. termed this network the "beloved community." When my twenty-two-year-old son forfeits the car for an evening so his sixteen-year-old brother can go on a date, or my eleven-year-old comforts her sister who has just scraped her shin, something mysterious lights our chaotic home. Something of the divine stirs here.

Children's first, best learning about God happens in the context of family. If that sounds arrogant, let's qualify. It doesn't mean the psalmist's idea of family, the olive branches placidly surrounding the table. Nor the hygienic, sentimentalized version of family often portrayed on television. It means family unsanitized, with all its warts.

From this muck can emerge fragrant lilacs; from the chaos of family life can spring religious faith. Children learn more from experiencing relationships than from studying doctrine. The Good News came first in the person of Jesus, not in a book. It continues to echo through human parents. Before we can trust an unseen God, we must first be able to trust visible, tangible human beings. From parents' touch, our response to the infant's needs, our laughter and wide embrace, the child learns that trust. Before children meet the larger faith community, they learn "community" at home: sorting laundry, negotiating TV channels, buying groceries with a fair distribution of treats.

We well know the difference between our public selves, who are far more polished (and to some extent, artificial) than the selves we reveal at home. Are we at our most authentic when seated in starched shirts around the office conference table? Or in robes around the kitchen table? While I may enjoy my work and find in it a sense of accomplishment, I suspect that I'm more the real "me" at home in jeans and sweatshirt. When people in retreat or counseling settings talk about their deepest concerns, it's usually not the spreadsheets or the sales figures. Job security may concern them, but the concern revolves around that primary sphere, the family.

A distinguished advisory board recently convened to discuss high risk, expensive publishing ventures. The professionals were businesslike at first, but gradually evolved into stories of "my William" and "what Sarah said when she was three." We repress parenthood when other tasks demand our attention, but eventually it emerges, sure as a Memphis accent or a passion for fly fishing.

People who honor home enough to explore its spirituality may get odd looks from their friends. Does this quirk mean they discuss liberation theology at dinner, or join their children in elaborate ritual celebrations? Not likely. It probably means that in the oddest corners of the house, they search for the sacred. Convinced that God dwells with us, they are intrigued by the surprising ways that presence pops up. In the bathroom or bedroom, the car or the garage, still and unseen, God seeks a dwelling place among human beings. Part II, "God in Surprising Places," describes the strange places where one family has found God, and may give others some clues on where to look. But the discovery is a uniquely personal one, which each family will make in its own way, in its own home.

— 4 —

THE PERPLEXED PARENT

O UR CHILDREN may well take the lead on this voyage into God. The parents are, if anything, the shakiest members of the crew. We want so badly to give our children what is best, but we seem paralyzed by insecurities and consumed with anxieties. Many of us have received neither adequate parenting nor adequate faith formation, yet we want our children's cups to overflow with both. We look into their faces and want them to be happy, holy, whole. Yet we know ourselves sadly deficient in all three areas.

To make matters worse, we live in a culture which does not value its children. Other industrialized nations have better schools and child-care policies than the United States. Every day in this country, more than 2,700 babies are born into poverty; more than 7,400 children are reported abused or neglected. One in five children lives below the poverty line; a child is killed by guns every two hours.[9]

In *High Tide in Tucson* Barbara Kingsolver describes a personal encounter with the discrepancies in cultural attitudes toward children. On her flight to Spain, another passenger on the plane put her own comfort first, rudely refusing to move over so Kingsolver's daughter could get some sleep. In contrast, as the mother and child stood on a bus in Spain, a man gently lifted the little girl into his seat. Kingsolver saw past his generosity to "the decades-old child, treasured by the manifold mothers of his neighborhood, growing up the way leavened dough rises surely to the kindness of bread."[10] In dramatic contrast, William Jarema proposes that many people in this country have had such poor nurturing, they walk around with an emptiness that looms like a hole in the chest.[11]

While many parents may not feel that bad about themselves, there are few thinking parents who don't question their roles. Knowing our inadequacies, it is reassuring to know God as father, mother, brother and sister, lover and friend. In prayer we can lift up our children to their creator and ask that our flaws be mended by the divine parent who never tires, grows crabby, or acts unjustly. Then the human part of us plugs away, hope restored, energy renewed.

My ambivalence about parenting was partly the result of my religious upbringing, but also partly my own fault. I wince at documents proclaiming that virginity is the primary call, the holier lifestyle. Every parent has at least once (usually while changing the sheets after the offspring get sick in the middle of the night) looked longingly at virginity as the easy, unencumbered way to sail through life. Finally I cringe at the statistics: 81 percent of the canonized saints in the Catholic calendar and 83 percent in the Episcopal are clerical or monastic.[12]

But the more painful work is examining my own attitudes. Surely they are influenced by official positions, but at my age, I have to take ownership and responsibility for my stance. Why do I, despite all I know to the contrary, still consider that church is a more privileged place than home, that a marble altar stands closer to God than the picnic table in the back yard? Why do I look to books for insights, when I know that the text of my own experience abounds in revelation?

Sometimes the exhaustion and multiple demands that seem to go with parenthood leave me too fuzzy to understand or appreciate anything, much less my chosen way of life. Furthermore, while many parents have personal mentors who have already raised their own kids, the traditional figure of resident grandma or grandpa, a storehouse of wise advice, is sadly missing from most nuclear families.

A recent example may clarify the state of my confusion. I'd been busy meeting with theologians, youth ministers, and catechists about the preparation of a resource for confirmation. We'd studied the rite, done theological reflection on its meaning, wrestled with ways to make the teaching relevant to teenagers. I don't mean to denigrate the importance of this work. The irony is that despite all this spirited academic preparation, I am still surprised when the Spirit puts in an appearance in a homely setting.

I picked up my youngest daughter after the day of meetings. On the way home, we had to stop by the insurance agent's office. I'd agreed to the errand that morning, before I realized that the day's schedule would balloon with unexpected phone calls and unscheduled crises. The usual rush-hour traffic was enough of an ordeal, but added to the chaos was a downpour so heavy that streets were flooding and passing cars were throwing massive walls of water into each other's paths.

The windshield wipers weren't working too effectively, the territory was unfamiliar, and my shoulders were tensely locked. "Help me out here, Hon," I cued my eleven-year-old navigator.

According to the teachings of my church, this child has not received the full outpouring of the Spirit in confirmation. But her empathetic action that day taught me about the Spirit's refusal to be confined by categories or age groupings. Knowing that I couldn't see street signs, she called out their names, told me when lights were turning, read the directions, counted the blocks to our destination.

Best of all, she kept up a steady massage of my shoulders, lifting the iron bar that burdened them, relaxing the stress on an old lady who'd put in a long day. No one asked her to do this; she knew the gesture instinctively. On a more typical day, she would have chattered about her activities. Today, she was wise enough to save the stories for a dry home at dinner.

She must have known that we were explorers together, struggling to find the insurance agent's office, and that sometimes adventure gets messy. Unasked, she simply rose to the occasion. It was not an unusual happening, and I'm sure that in homes and offices, courts and hospitals around the city that day, parents and children did equally splendid things. But I use this example because it is so ordinary, because in the routine we take for granted simmers a holiness that can knock our socks off. Furthermore, *anyone* can find such examples if only one knows where to look.

I am hesitant to put theological language on such grace and simplicity. So I will simply say that a rush-hour drive through a rainstorm can call forth heroism, that in the circumstances we least expect it to emerge, God's presence comes. We who are busily craning our necks into tabernacles and tomes may well miss the dazzling brilliance of the ordinary. If we aren't alert to the fact that God visits us at home, then we are likely to be unwelcoming hosts and hostesses, gawking elsewhere. Parents should take seriously the words of Meister Eckhart: "God is at home. It is we who have gone out for a walk."[13]

Perhaps experiencing the love of a parent for a child comes as close as humans can to knowing how God loves us. Between God and us, as between parent and child stretches a vast chasm. But as Thornton Wilder wrote, "The bridge is love, the only survival, the only meaning."[14] I've been privileged to walk that bridge.

When she was three, Katie used to turn my face away from my computer, thrust the keyboard aside, and plop squarely into my lap. She was a tough teacher, but her lesson stuck. The projects can be placed on hold; the child is the immediate grace, the bearer of God in our midst. Grubby and insistent, my children have helped me appreciate that through Jesus, God wrapped himself in skin, becoming

— 5 —

THE TIES THAT BIND

YOU'D THINK after four tries, I'd get it right. But one parenting skill that still remains a mystery is the art of the papoose wrap. It begins early in the parenting career. Exhausted and sore, a new mother lies in her hospital bed awaiting the baby's first visit after the clean-up. In that mysterious interlude between the delivery room and the hospital bed, competent nurses efficiently scrub off the vernix, wash the bloody, matted hair, and generally make a naked, wailing creature presentable to the parents.

They also encase the infant in a blanket wrap so meticulous that it makes computer software design look sloppy. Those ramrod-straight folds and precision corners intimidate new parents who are still wondering why they ever got themselves into this pickle. The baby books reinforce the inferiority complex by reminding us that the infant was tightly enclosed in the womb and craves the same security in tight swaddling clothes. If a fist pokes out or a toe escapes, we'll probably pay therapists forever.

Maternity floor rumor has it that some parents check out early to get home, unwrap their child and find out if he or she has all ten toes! (We're too terrified to try it in the hospital. If Maternity Ward Drill Sergeant ever caught us, or scornfully saw our pathetic rewrap job, she might recognize rookies and forbid us to escape with our precious, albeit badly bundled, little one.)

Little did I dream then that I'd spend the rest of my life exploring the tight wrap and weave of parenthood. Elizabeth Ann Seton, a single mother of five, said it all in the nineteenth century: "Children so wind themselves round one's heart as to almost make one wonder how existence could be supportable without them." Not only would existence become insupportable; it would lack a whole dimension. It is almost as if we live our lives twice and, in so doing, increase our capacity for empathy. Recently, events in my children's lives have struck resonances with events in mine, as though a great gong echoes on some quivering air current between us.

As our oldest son finishes college, the triumph of graduation is tempered by wondering, "What's next?" At the same time, I switched from a teaching career to one in writing and publishing. Fortunately, old friends eased the transition by acting like personal cheerleaders. They reminded me that no matter where the career path led, I stood squarely in their affections.

The echoes were almost deafening as David asked me to rehearse an important job interview. "How do I talk about my strengths without boasting? What weaknesses can I admit, without jeopardizing the job?" I tried to give him the same steady reassurance my friends had given me. "If this job doesn't work out, there's a better one in store. Go into that interview confident. You don't have to grovel to these people. You know you're good."

Eight years before, David had gone through the wavering confidence stage of a nerdy eighth grader. All the encouragement from home meant little, however, compared to winning a first place trophy in a speech meet. When he brought home that surprise, I bought him a navy blue T-shirt with big white letters that read, "Damn, I'm good."

No matter how old we grow or how successful we are, we seem to crave that reminder. Beneath the gowns of doctoral candidates, prominent surgeons, and Supreme Court judges, does the T-shirt slogan whisper? The poet Peter Meinke captured this deep human need in a poem for his son:

> I thought you knew
> you were beautiful and fair
> your bright eyes and hair
> but now I see that no one knows that
> about himself, but must be told
> and retold until it takes hold
> because I think anything can be killed
> after a while, especially beauty.... [16]

Seeing my own job struggles mirrored in my son, it was as if they took on a separate dimension that demanded a different perspective. Faith may tell us that we are dear to God, that our identity is rooted in being the apple of God's eye, but we still need to hear that affirmation in human voices, the message mediated by caring eyes and warm hands. All the lofty abstractions in the world sometimes mean less than a phrase over the phone, a line in a letter, a slogan on a T-shirt.

People without children seem to spend lots of time getting in touch with their inner child. People with children have direct access to that little person who surfaces mysteriously from the past into the present. She may wear different styles and speak a different lingo, but her joys and struggles carry us back thirty years to the metallic surfaces of swings and slides, the barren landscape of a lonely playground, the classroom smells of dust and chalk.

People with many children often have a depth that must come from living many lives. They've revisited the normal human capacity for joy and heartache, the whole broad gamut of experience, several times over!

We may deliver a baby, but we never separate completely from that life that has been so much a part of ours. Just as the bloodstream and food supplies once intermingled, now we connect in less tangible ways. We may no longer worry about alcohol or nicotine crossing the placenta, but kids' stresses still show up in our bodies: *our* stomach ache during *their* driving test, *our* pain during *their* penicillin shot, *our* headache as *their* fever mounts.

It must be some bizarre compensation for those of us who never figured out the papoose wrap. We may have flunked Swaddling 101, but we spend the rest of our days inextricably tangled. Maybe it's the memory of that baby powder fragrance, the utter dependence of that tiny creature that keeps us forever bound. Maybe it's the experience of leading intertwined lives. Whatever the cause, it enlarges our hearts past the bursting point, makes us bigger than we ever thought we could become. Whatever the reason, the old song was right: "Blessed be the ties that bind."

— 6 —

GOD OF MOUNTAINS AND SEA

WHEN WE GAZE at the Pacific Ocean, the Rocky Mountains, or the Milky Way, we're overwhelmed by immensity. Such scenes offer only a peek at the awesome mystery of God. Children and parents alike need a sense of the sacred, a tabernacle before which to bow and learn how small humans are in relationship to the divine.

Sometimes I think, "Ah — I've caught some flash of God's hem. Through some peak experience, I've glimpsed the Holy One." But at the same time, "I ain't seen nothing yet." When I am drawn deeply into prayer, when I am suffused with love for another, when I stand transfixed before beauty, it's only the beginning. Endless as ocean waves, God's love beckons on and on. Then on some more.

It's not easy to translate infinity into language for children. To them I say, "God is full of surprises." I teach them a gesture-prayer to begin each morning. Standing with hands open, cupped, and outstretched tells God, "You'll send marvelous surprises today. Alert me to your hide-and-seek tactics, your presence in unexpected places."

Another specific way to approach this vastness is to spend time in whatever beauties nature provides locally: a city park or botanic gardens, a river or meadow. Because we live in Colorado, we go skiing in the Rockies. Like many adventures, it begins with hassles. In a long and grueling process, we cram the car with skis, boots, poles, mittens, hats, and paraphernalia for everyone. When it is bulging with kids and equipment, we drive west, often as the mountains glow with the pink reflection of dawn.

On the first run I sink into a content as deep as the powder. I swish through corridors of pine, with the froth of mountains billowing on the horizons. To the right, they pile like ocean waves on each other. To the left, granite rises in a perfectly symmetrical cone shape against a sky so blue, so clear I have seen it only at this high altitude.

In such a setting, I glide silkily down the slope, imagining a sundae: hot fudge melting down vanilla ice cream. A certain confidence comes from knowing a mountain: its broad back, its forgiving snow, its blue-shadowed hollows. For a few, rare moments throughout the day, there is a lull between skiers, and I am alone with the mountain.

At other times, I ski with the children — when they want a rest and slow down enough to join me! Then, in a burst of energy, we belt out Calypso songs or Christmas carols to the startled jays. The children, after all, got me into this: coaxing an old lady to come with them because they knew how much I would like it, and might then be more inclined to pay their way. In the early days, when my anxiety was intense, they would ski close beside me, calling out encouragement: "Are you sure you haven't been on skis all your life?" "Excuse me, ma'am, but are you training for the Olympics?" "Sharp turn, Mom! Try taking it a little faster...." Even now a thinly disguised note of desperation creeps in: "Could you please speed up?"

If ever I am stuck in an antiseptic hospital room, I will recall our days on the slopes: the snow squeaking beneath our skis, the air crisp with pine, the confetti of colorful jackets dotting the vast white expanses. All the senses are alert while the body finds its rhythms: turning and shifting weight as if to an inner music. Skiing has the distinct hallmark of any physical activity: the less I think about it, the better I do.

Sometimes early in the morning, we are the first down a powdery trail. I follow my older daughter as we carve a series of perfect Ss in the snow. Looking back, our paths are indistinguishable: it is impossible to tell who leads, who follows. With a stretch of the imagination, it is the perfect image for mutuality.

My relationship with Colleen is, I suspect, not unlike that of any mother with a young adult daughter. High school brought a roller coaster of ups and downs, but now we have reached a wonderful plateau where we can enjoy a shopping trip, a Chinese lunch, and an Irish poet like the best of friends. In the past year, she has introduced me to new fashions, new writers, and new music that have immensely enriched middle age. How stodgy I might have become without her!

So what does that have to do with God? Perhaps just another bit of evidence of how precisely God gives us what we need. On ski terrain that stretches for four thousand acres trivial concerns are forgotten. Easily and enthusiastically, we enter the broad realm of a gracious God. We remember who we are: children in our father's spacious mansion.

A similar experience occurred when we visited Sanibel Island, Florida, which has some of the finest shelling beaches in the world. The visit proved that God does not limit revelation to one particular latitude or geographical zone. What occurred on that tropical island could also come in a field of corn or wheat, beneath a starry sky, beside a lake, on marshes, prairies, or deserts.

Why? Because it was an experience of profusion, which could occur as snow crystals pirouette in the sparkly air, as we plunge into a bounteous meal or inhale the fragrance of fresh bread, as we think of all the people who have blessed our lives. It could occur as we consider the 50 billion galaxies spotted by the Hubble telescope, or the countless varieties of cormorants, snowy egrets, ibis, and osprey, flocks so huge that at one time in history, they blotted out the sun.

The sheer bounty of creation is so staggering that to appreciate it at all we must focus on one tiny segment. Here on Sanibel, a profligate creator spills sun on white beaches, tosses palm trees gracefully along the shore, lays mountains of shells. If there were only one, we'd be stunned by its beauty. Here they are piled hundreds deep, so that the tides turning them create a tinkling, watery music. If indeed beauty is a door to the sacred, this threshold is wide and inviting.

Until I returned home, I did not know that such excursions into plenty had a technical theological name. Then, with the "ah ha!" of recognition, I read Richard Rohr's *Radical Grace*. He maintains that people who spend their energies avoiding the "near occasions of sin," should instead plant themselves in the "near occasions of grace."[17]

So a walk through a forest, a weekend at a farm, or a stroll along a beach is a much more profound experience than the "vacation getaway" advertised by the airlines. That serene, empty space which we enter ourselves and share with our children is a potent invitation to the play of grace. When we leave behind the ledgers of tight schedules and the anxieties of bank accounts, we take the first steps toward our own liberation.

Running onto the beach for the first time, Katie wants to gather all the shells into arms that could never hold such abundance. Proudly, she aligns her finds on the porch and matches them to the charts kindly provided on the grocery store sacks. (Sanibel may be the only place in the world where the commercial messages we expect on white plastic bags are replaced by the intricate designs of shark's eye and sailor's ear, calico scallop and angel wing, lace murex and pear whelk, coquina and egg cockle....)

Who could conceive both the vast seascape and the microscopic detail of a shell tinier than Katie's freckle? Even the hint of such a span can fill us with a rich serenity: We too are held in masterful hands. We too participate in plenty. When we are steeped in such abundance, we can ignore the trivia, or at least deal with it blithely, handle the junk knowing there is far more of treasure.

The people we meet here seem to have an unflappable security, perhaps because most of them are retired. For Katie it is a paradise of grandmas and grandpas, who share their sandy finds and praise her discoveries. The trading of shells appears to be one of the social rites of Sanibel: simple, direct, graceful. Katie also helps to heft errant crabs back into the sea, and shares triumphant high fives with her elderly conspirators: they have saved lives today! Her bare back is dusted with a light frosting of sand, like a sugar cookie.

At the shell museum, we listen absorbed to a grandpa steeped in shell lore. In his warm brown eyes, I recognize the recipient of a blessing Rachel Carson once asked:

> If I had influence with the good fairy who is supposed to preside over the christening of all children, I should ask that her gift to each child in the world be a sense of wonder so indestructible that it would last throughout life, as an unfailing antidote against boredom and disenchantments of later years, the sterile preoccupation with things that are artificial, the alienation from the sources of our strength.[18]

I breathe a silent prayer that each of my children might find in the natural order some fascination that will keep their wonder alive as long as life lasts. Not that they must all become marine biologists or astronomers, but as they pursue their careers as journalists, pediatricians, or economists, they can breathe the scent of blue spruce, pause for the rich enjoyment of a flame-colored salvia or an earthy-toned sparrow, savor the citrus pearls of an orange segment. Surely in the bounty that surrounds us lies refuge from cynicism, apathy, and despair. Surely God speaks as clearly through creation as through a sermon in church or a book in the library, and attentiveness to the natural world can be a form of prayer.

We return home to sullen skies and frigid temperatures. Yet we do not enter winter without our talismans. Strewn in suitcases, tucked into shoes, and curled in cuffs are the shells. They float through the wash and tumble in the drier. Discovering these random treasures, we know what Terry Tempest Williams meant in *Refuge*, "I blow on these images like the last burning embers on a winter's night."[19]

Research in our land-locked library turns up intriguing discoveries: the shell was the symbol of the pilgrim, and an early picture of St. James shows him with a scallop on his staff. Our trip, it turns out, could take its place in a longer line: the pilgrimages to Compostela, Canterbury, Rome. Did those medieval pilgrims taste the same abundance, return with the same treasures?

I hope that during some boring class, Katie reaches into the pocket of her sweatshirt, fingers a yellow cockle, a king's crown, or a kitten's paw, imagines hibiscus crimson against a lapis sky, remembers abundance, and smiles mysteriously to herself. That may be one of the most profound lessons in theology that she will ever absorb.

_ 7 _

GOD OF TRANSFORMATION

W HEN WE TAKE the long view of the parenting process, we can
see the gradual transformations it entails: both for the kids
and for us.

Parents may also be able to see the sacred more clearly in the lives
of our children than in our own. As tightly as we are bound to them,
they are still *other*. We share intensely in their moments of triumph,
but they are not *our* moments. The child who receives an award or a
degree invested considerable amounts of his or her own time and tal-
ent in it. We may have been the cheerleaders, but we didn't cross the
finish line. We allow ourselves to swell with pride precisely because
it's not our achievement; we tend to be more humble and realistic
about what we attain ourselves.

Being so close to another, yet being distinct gives us a unique perspective on a process which parallels our own growth into Christ.
During a diaper change, few parents imagine a day when they will
share their coffee and their inmost thoughts with this little person.
Yet many parents eventually experience the phenomenon of their
child becoming one of their best friends. Clarissa Pinkola Estes writes
that "a grown daughter is also a sister."[20] The transformation is
doubly delightful when we recall bitter arguments over curfews and
grades a few short years ago. Not without irony, I ask my young
adult son and daughter their viewpoints on issues affecting their
siblings, who are now in the same difficult adolescent years they
endured not long ago.

If parenting is about anything, it is about transformation. We
know personally the dramatic difference a shower can make after
a hot, dusty road trip, or a how a good night's sleep can cure the
crabbiness after a bout of insomnia. When we turn from ourselves
to our children, we are stunned by the daily miracle, which we miss
more often than not. Over time, a tiny, dependent infant who can't
even hold up her wobbly head turns into the gracious young woman
addressing the graduates. "It flew too fast!" we think at such threshold times, and surely some of the tears shed at weddings are due to
the fact that we can't quite understand where the toddlers have gone.

Sometimes it takes the more objective viewpoint of another adult to alert us to time's transformative effects. Fortunately, we receive this reality check annually, when we vacation at the lakeside home of an old friend. He and his wife recently celebrated their fiftieth wedding anniversary; they are the parents of five and the grandparents of many more children. Over a period of fifteen years, they have watched our children grow from infants to toddlers to young adults.

Their special favors are poured on our youngest daughter. It tends to mystify the other children: Why does Katie get the home-made ice cream, the ride on the tractor or horse? Knowing the sorrows of the older couple, I have some inkling. When they look wistfully at our daughters, they must be remembering their daughters. One died of leukemia; another was killed in a car crash. Their other daughter and two sons thrived, but the hole in the heart must still ache.

One day, the old gentleman articulated that sadness. We had just arrived, and during his usual glad reunion with Katie, he marvelled at her growth over the previous year. Then he turned to her parents, a secondary interest, but a necessary appendage for the children's visit. "Seeing your kids again," he said, "it's like a dream remembered. A dream remembered. Someday you'll look at each other and say, 'Where have the children gone?' "

Throughout the rest of our stay, I watched the children more keenly, well aware that our vacation days were limited. I tried to imprint the details on my senses as they hiked through fragrant meadows and paddled canoes through rippling waters. Knowing that the time would come too soon when jobs and other commitments would prevent us all from being on the lake together, I wanted to hold tight to the memories.

Perhaps I knew unconsciously that the only way to appreciate the process is to focus on a few turning points. Otherwise, it gets away from us, in the hurry of daily scheduling and the press of ordinary detail. We find ourselves in the sorry position of John Hubbel writing in *Goodbye, My Son,* "Then he was gone. And it was over much too soon."

Each family has its own landmarks, but a common watershed must be the events that cluster around graduations and kids starting independent lives. It is rare to have a chapter of our shared story end with a symbolic drum roll or trumpet crescendo. So when one came at David's high school graduation, we paid attention.

After four years of prodding and struggle, of waking up early for exams and staying up late for study sessions, he was finally graduating from a Jesuit high school. David's easygoing ways and their strict discipline had not always meshed, and we were regular attendees at coerced parent-teacher conferences.

Naturally, the family felt some nervousness as we filled our row in the gym for graduation. We watched attentively as a long line of faculty and graduates filed into the ceremony and a brass quintet played "Pomp and Circumstance." Following all the dignitaries came one lone figure in red cap and gown: our son. He mounted the stage, walked to the podium, and began: "Welcome to the 114th commencement exercises. As president of the senior class, I have the honor of being master of ceremonies today."

Our pride swelled close to bursting as he thanked the dignitaries and introduced the speakers. But I had already rehearsed that part of the script with him. The surprise came when he invited a hundred classmates to stand and face their parents.

"Now," he said, "let's applaud the people who made this possible." Across a thousand heads, his gaze sought ours. His smile spoke a gratitude no words could touch. At that moment, I knew how lovely a launching could be.

After the elation of graduation, his college send-off was Kleenex Day. Nothing in ten years of college teaching had prepared me to view the scene through a parent's eyes. David looked sad and forlorn as I left him with a stack of boxes in a closet-sized dorm room. Once before, when he'd entered kindergarten, I'd heartlessly left him at the door. I had a hunch that parenthood was a series of wrenching goodbyes, but this one was a dramatic step in the unraveling of our family life.

That fabric had at times been woven so close it chafed, and I'd longed for an end to pacifiers, sibling fights, lost retainers, and a phone I could never use. But now I would've given anything for a toddler to potty-train. I agreed fully with the comic strip character comforting his wife as she cleaned up another mess created by the kids: "First they break your things, and then they break your heart."

I would have to learn to start dinner without the usual cue: David's agonized yelp at the front door, "Ma! I'm starving! Feed me!" I would even have to cope without his buddies, those acned, awkward adolescents who traveled in packs, devouring any crumb of food not locked in cupboards. I would also be surprised by the impact of his leaving on the rest of the family. That first morning, Katie left for second grade in tears, wailing, "But I only had him for seven years!" I joined her, weeping, "I only had him for nineteen!"

Now who would rub my back after a tense day? Who would drive

Katie to soccer and Sean to the pet store? Who would be Colleen's
confidante and co-conspirator? Who would dispel tension with a
joke and defuse a dinnertime crisis with a well-timed burp? The family configuration was shifting, and I was sadly reminded by the lone
bagel left in the refrigerator, the pair of boxers forgotten in the ham-
per. I had glimpsed the heart of a God who longs desperately for her
children, misses their humor, likes their noise, and aches for the sight
of them. This God is the father of the parable, who peers intently
down an empty road, yearning for the vanished child.

In the initial misery, I never anticipated the joys that hovered beyond the threshold. Perhaps the most practical change was a decrease
in Mom's domestic load. Now I had more time for the younger
children and my own projects. Realizing how fast our days together would go, I changed some priorities, making sure we had
time to catch crickets for Sean's lizard or snuggle up with Katie's
favorite book.

I was learning the truth of the Buddhist saying that every hello
contains the seeds of goodbye, and every goodbye contains the seeds
of hello. If parents do not close one door, they miss the bright potential of opening another. Had I not endured the forlorn farewell
to David his first day of college, I would never have seen him as
student body president, in cap and gown, addressing the opening
convocation two years later.

Had I not waved a weepy goodbye to an airplane hurtling down
the runway when my daughter left for college, I could never have
read her Mother's Day letter that brought joyous tears nine months
later. A little distance from home gave her an appreciation of the
family she would not have had as a permanent resident.

In this mixture of goodbyes and hellos, I have seen God lifting the
divine hands from creation. Poised in the air for a terrible moment,
those hands grant us freedom. Just as a potter raises her hands from
the finished bowl, so God must step back and breathe a long "Ah!"
My young adults are now full of youthful energy and potential as
they balance on a threshold where the future stretches mysteriously
before them.

My instinct is to hover protectively, but like God, I must sometimes say, "Hands off." They must own their lives, the mistakes as
well as the triumphs. Participating in this paradox, I learn how God's
constant care can be intertwined with the gift of independence.

As for the future, I'm hesitant to venture onto ground I have not
yet explored. But I have a hunch that what lies before us now is
learning to relate as adults to adults. My friends with older chil-

dren seem to have discovered innovative ways to remain connected even as they have successfully let go. There's a blessed humor in the process. Writer and family-life expert Dolores Curran laughs as she recounts a scuba-diving expedition with her grown son and daughter. She emerged from the water just in time to hear Teresa tell her brother, "You watch Mom now. I'll take care of Dad."

The roles may reverse and the dance steps may change, but the underlying affection remains constant. I vividly remember the look on my dad's face when he met his first grandchild, in a fuzzy yellow snowsuit at the St. Louis airport.

My uncle's eyes had the same glow as he watched his son feed his own infant on a porch in Boston. We've all seen the pride clothing the parents of the graduate or the bride and groom. In their elation, we capture the wonder of God, surveying all creation and finding it good.

If my children's transformations have been dramatic, mine have been no less stunning. If I were to meet the "me" of the prechildren days, I doubt that I'd find her too interesting. "What a bookish, self-centered sort *she* is!" I'd probably say. "Organized and punctual, precise to a T — but how shallow, how intolerant! What would we ever have in common?"

It has been one of life's great graces that I gave birth to my children once, and they've been birthing me ever since. More than twenty years ago, I'd met a squawking bundle in a hospital delivery room, but didn't have the slightest idea how to care for him. The sixth-grade class I taught at the time had kindly showered me with baby supplies, but learning how to use the stuff was strictly trial and error. Since then we'd encountered plenty of crises, catastrophes, drudgeries and triumphs. Subtly, they had left their marks, proving, if nothing else, that "this too will pass."

The whole process reminds me of a scene in the movie *Romero*. After the intellectual, detached archbishop experiences the violence of Salvadoran soldiers, he is numb and shocked. He stands paralyzed, naked to the waist, until his people approach, place a stole around his shoulders, and encourage him to say Mass. Under their touch, his identity is restored.

Under the influence of my children, I have become a person I never anticipated. If a child's survival depends on our response, we rise to the occasion. Answering children's needs, we become people of larger vision, less intent on our pleasures than on their nurture.

In this transformation, our children work in partnership with God. God has a dream for each of us, which includes becoming less selfish, more giving of self. As we struggle toward that goal, our children unconsciously become our best coaches.

They view us not as bank accounts or food sources but as wide laps and warm embraces. We meet their expectations, becoming the safe harbors they crave and offering them wings for flight. They call forth our finest selves and bring us back to earth if we get too uppity. One mom who worked hard at bringing her children close to God laughed at her own efforts. "When I get too pompous," she said, "the kids let me know. One of them flipped me off. Another one mooned me."

Trying not to become too serious about it, we do enflesh for our children the divine parent. We do things for our children that defy our limitations and deepen our loves. When we meet the challenges of the flu, the spelling homework, the science fair project, or the prom dress, we act like the God who would do anything for us.

Any parent who's honest about the constant demands on time and energy admits, "I never knew I could do it." Indeed, with the grace of God, we do more than we ever dreamed we could. Our homes are filled with proof of Revelation 21:5: "Behold, I make all things new."

PART II

God in Surprising Places

If we believe God is everywhere, then no place is without that supportive presence. When parents and children start searching for God, it can make a scavenger hunt look tame: the more unusual the hiding place, the better the chances of finding God there. These chapters describe unexpected places where one family has found God — a castle, cafeteria, and concert, a dentist and driving lesson — but they are not the final word. Rather than being a one-size-fits-all template, this section should prompt readers to ask, "In what surprising places do we find God?"

— 8 —

GOD (SOMEWHERE HERE) IN THE CLUTTER

WE MAKE A MISTAKE if we think of God like a snooty guest who visits our home only if it's clean. Jesus seemed to drop in on his friends unannounced, and the only one who complained was Martha. This scriptural nugget only reinforced my natural domestic laziness and influenced me to quit reading women's magazines. Their glossy photos of meticulously placed pillows, color-coordinated towels and meals arranged like works of art were just too intimidating. On better days, we cleared a path through the house, found a dry towel (its color coding secondary to its relative cleanliness), and more or less threw together three meals. No need to pay money for nasty reminders of our inadequacies, I deduced, even without the services of a shrink.

The avoidance technique worked until I spent a weekend living in a Better Home. My hostess was an old friend with the soul of an artist. It goes without saying that she and her husband are also childless. Cynically, I envisioned that lovely Victorian home at the mercy of a toddler. The oil paintings propped on easels? Crash! The lavish eyelet draperies in the bathroom? Splash! The delicate works of art displayed on every end table? Smithereens! Even I walked on tip-toe and paid attention where I put down my water glass. If they had posted "Don't Touch" signs, the message couldn't have been clearer: I was sojourning in a museum.

Ever the clod, I made the faux pas of carrying my kitchen wine glass into the dining room, assuming with maternal economy, "one size fits all." Ah, no. As my host courteously whisked away the offending goblet, he whispered, "You have a *kitchen* wine glass." It looked fine to me — until I saw the replacement: Waterford spun from crystals, faceted brilliantly as diamonds. I mustered the dignity of the Queen Mother to sip from it.

With the same awe, I sniffed the vase of hyacinths beside my bed and the potpourri tucked in my pillow. Stroking the filigreed pen conveniently placed beside the artistic note paper, I tried to forget how we scratched memos on the back of absence slips, delighted to unearth even an unsharpened eyebrow pencil. A guest room stocked with lavender bubble bath? We thought we were doing well when we changed the sheets on the extra bed! I suppressed further memories of home in order to twirl like a ballerina through this forty-eight-hour bubble of aesthetic delights.

As if in retaliation, the awkward realities of home hit me hard when I returned through the fog of jet lag. I did not deal regally with the Monday morning chorus after my homecoming:

"Mom, I'm out of socks!"

"Sew the button on my pants, or I'll go to school bottomless!"

And the ultimate threat: "If you don't sign my permission slip, you'll have to chaperone the field trip!"

After the kids tumbled out the door, more or less intact, I collapsed with a cup of coffee and a burden of guilt. Why couldn't we preserve some tattered shred of the weekend graciousness? Would Sean's teacher notice the blob of glue on his slacks? Could Katie make it through the day concealing her unmatched socks?

The self-criticism took on a shriller note as I contemplated my surroundings. Clutter filled every surface I saw. Precariously high piles teetered on the dining room table, and I winced to think that somewhere in there lurked the tax forms, the manuscript due last week, and the errant permission slip. The whole scene screamed out for attention — probably not so much from a museum curator as from a burly bulldozer operator.

Readers who are beginning to recognize their own domestic junk heaps will be relieved to know that I didn't plunge into cleaning. Guilt motivates only as far as an initial sweep across the desk. Then the writer takes over, playing with the nuances, lassoing the words to mine this experience as assiduously as my artist friend arranged the flowers. Maybe it's just an elaborate exercise in rationalizing a family of slobs, but I'd rather think it's an attempt to find God, somewhere here in the clutter.

The first encouraging hint came from a closer look at those piles. One contained all the research for a report on crocodiles. Prompted by a school project on an endangered species, we'd chosen this one because we'd almost pulled the car off the road in Florida when we drove past the sign "Gator Crossing." Over the last several weeks, we'd been steeped in a crocodile soup of National Geographic documentaries, library books, and statistics. Furthermore, we'd all cheered when our fifth grader completed the first report she'd typed (albeit painstakingly, with the two-fingered poke) into the computer.

What to the casual observer would look like a messy stack of papers, discs, and books could be seen more sympathetically as a pinnacle of achievement, a swaying tower celebrating learning.

Okay, maybe that's a stretch, but other evidence contributed to the rationale that all this stuff was indeed evidence of lively activity: the rugby shorts and letters from friends, the basketball and souvenirs, the birthday party favors and magazines. The calendar (if I could find it) bulged with commitments and coming events; the phone machine was chock full of messages. At one point in my checkered domestic career, I had in desperation posted a sign, "Dull people have immaculate homes." Oldest son, reading it, replied, "Well then, we must be really interesting!" (Slobs have highly refined defense mechanisms....)

A friend with five kids who had long ago made her peace with something less than a House Beautiful once consoled me when I was bogged down with four cases of chicken pox and was losing my mind to laundry. "Hey, when we go to heaven," she said, "God will only ask two questions: 'Did you love the people I gave you to love? Did you appreciate the gifts I put into your life?'"

Sure, I messed up on the socks now and then, but all four kids knew they were loved and, most of the time, were happy. How could anyone *not* value such fragile gifts more than the Louis XIV side table? Maybe we didn't scour it often, but we did appreciate our home, with its overflowing bookshelves, ample kitchen, and cottonwoods arching over a yard big enough for soccer games. It would be a sorry spectacle to a decorator, but the scruffy pots on the window sills had an awkward charm, blooming with bulbs planted by kid fists.

Somehow a casual attitude toward cleaning had rubbed off on youngest daughter. When I gave Katie an elaborate description of the Kleenex basket in my friend's home, lined with starched white doilies and tied with bows in the same shade as the tissues, she fired back, directly and uniquivocally, "Your friend has way too much time on her hands." An interesting set of values I've passed on, huh?

Sometimes nothing clarifies an understanding better than a story. Luckily, it was shortly after my venture into Artistic Lifestyles that I came across an English tale recorded by Megan McKenna.[21] The king, it seems, wanted to be an expert archer. After dedicated practice and persistent discipline, he achieved 75 percent accuracy. After further work with a Zen guru, he perfected his aim and concentration, improving his mark to 90 percent — with his eyes closed!

But the king was pained because he couldn't get better. He fretted because he couldn't surpass this astonishing level of achievement....

Then one day he traveled through a village where he was amazed to see barn after barn on which were targets filled with arrows quivering dead center! Here, he knew, lived a master. Who, it turned out, was a young boy under twelve. At first the child felt shy, but he agreed to teach the king everything he knew about archery.

They began by practicing technique, shooting arrows into the barn wall. Then, to the king's absolute disbelief, the boy grabbed his bucket and paint, and drew the target around the arrows. "That's how I do it!" he smiled lopsidedly. "I get 100 percent when I paint the target on afterward." The king, at first stunned and humiliated, then angry, finally burst out laughing.

And so must all parents who recognize themselves in that approach. When we get into a dither about our failures, our children remind us to simply adjust the target. Sometimes we focus myopically on the wrong goal: if in pursuit of the immaculate home, we scream at its residents, we've wandered off the mark. In all the recorded words of Jesus, there's not one about the polished kitchen floor. But there are several mentions of his welcoming the children, who in first-century Palestine acted as they would in twentieth-century Colorado, probably crawling over him with grubby hands, runny noses, and stained shirts.

Someday another family would live in our house, but surely the days we'd spent, the meals we'd eaten, and the ways we'd loved would live on. While our stay may have been messy, the house has contained an abundant life that will continue through our children and friends.

I'm still fond of a world with tinkling background music and aesthetic delights in every corner. For a weekend, I relish royalty. But I also like to move into the world where I take up permanent residence. Coming home. Painting the target around the arrow. Seeking God in the clutter.

— *9* —

THE SUPER CITIZEN AWARD

N OW AND THEN, the most disorderly household fills with joy. Parents at our children's elementary school have a once-in-a-year chance to participate in a monthly ritual, conducted with the utmost secrecy. The principal telephones parents in advance; they cancel prior commitments and change their schedules to accommodate the Event; whispered conversations swirl around the preparations of camera, flash, and film. When her teacher calls that morning, I lie to my daughter, "Oh, it was just someone wanting a donation." To preserve the secrecy, the most blatant lie is justified.

At the school that afternoon, the parents are hidden away in the principal's office, then smuggled to a side entrance of the gym where the whole school is assembled. As each honoree's name is called, the parents appear in a grand reunion scene reminiscent of "This Is Your Life." (Never mind that we've been separated for an arduous three hours or so. . . .) Handshakes, certificates, T-shirts, photos, applause all around. In this scene of unmitigated shlock, no one beams more proudly than the mother of the super citizen.

Will I list it first in my obituary? Will this moment take precedence over my college scholarship, writing awards, silver bowl from the university alumnae, podium before audiences around the country? It just might. My daughter's award-winning moment has, of course, a history. And because of my peculiar bent for practical theology, it told me much about God.

It all began when I returned from Phoenix. There I'd given a workshop on the sacraments of initiation, which actually became a cheerleading session for the wonderful things that catechists were doing there. Hesitantly they explained how parents and children had carved images of God from clay. "Then," said Jesusita almost apologetically. "I forgot the stool for the kids to wash their hands. But it was a good mistake. The parents wound up kneeling before their children, washing the clay from their hands."

Hearing her story about the simple gestures of care, I could have packed up my overheads, charts, and hand-outs. I wanted to genuflect in reverence before the catechists of Phoenix and hop on the next plane home. What could I possibly add to their stories? They knew more about the sacraments of the ordinary than I could ever teach. I flew back to Denver with euphoria and admiration.

Then I read Katie's Religion test (that combination of terms becoming increasingly an oxymoron for me). "Baptism: A Sacrament of Welcome," the title chirped. That cheery heading was quickly contradicted by her grade. Scrawled in red pen beneath the welcome banner was "63 – F." Oddly enough, one of her mistakes was a matching question on which she had connected chrism with "sign of the Holy Spirit."

Now I'm no expert, but I had just participated in a ritual where the catechists of Phoenix anointed each other. I'd suggested that two or three demonstrate the ritual, but, oh, no: everyone got into the act. As I dashed around refilling from a squirt bottle of baby oil mixed with rose perfume, they lavished each other with words of encouragement for their ministries. The words of a song, "You are anointed in Christ. It is he that you have put on," played softly on the tape recorder as the room filled with fragrance and presence. Maybe I'd flunk a test on which person of the Trinity showed up, but I could've sworn it was the Spirit.

When I politely questioned Katie's teacher about the discrepancy, she explained that she merely followed the answer key that came with the text book. To her credit, she consulted the parish staff, and their consternation was quick and on target. How could the Religion text contradict the liturgical catechesis of abundant oil lavished on the newly baptized and witnessed by the children of the parish? We were quick to select another resource for faith formation.

But that wasn't the end of the story. When Katie's birthday rolled around soon after the debacle of the Religion test, she took Rice Krispies treats to school. "Who did you ask to help you pass them out?" I asked, remembering from older children that this was an important part of the birthday ceremony.

"I asked the kids no one ever asks," she replied nonchalantly. "Max and Leah." I almost choked on my coffee. She had named the two children ostracized as surely as if they carried leprosy. Max hurled books across the classroom in fits of rage, struck out at any child or teacher dumb enough to get close, and locked himself in the closet, where he sampled everyone's lunch. Leah was a scrawny, pathetic child whose mousiness seemed to blend into the white boards.

I had always believed Walker Percy's dictum, "It is possible to get As in Religion and flunk life."[22] Now Katie had demonstrated the inverse: "It is possible to flunk Religion and get As in life." How unselfconsciously she had lived out a baptismal commitment in the same week she'd flunked the test on it.

I was not the only one who noticed. Her teacher awarded her with Super Citizen that month, the long story that had brought us to this moment. As I waited in the wings, I thought of Jesus saying at the Last Supper: "The one who believes in me will also do the works that I do and in fact, will do greater works than these" (John 14:12). Until I had children, I never understood those words. How could the bumbling disciples whom he addressed surpass the miracles, the compassion, the self-sacrifice of their master?

Even more intriguing is the conviction in Jesus' tone of voice. He knew himself what it meant to be restricted by the false limitations imposed by other people. The residents of his hometown asked, "Where did this man get this wisdom and these deeds of power? Is not this the carpenter's son? Is not his mother called Mary?" (Matt. 13:54–55) Because they refused to allow him greatness and insisted on boxing him into a narrow niche, he did not do many miracles there. His example demonstrates how a climate of high expectations is optimal for people to flourish.

Children who are lavishly praised and encouraged show how achievement thrives in a positive climate. While my stories may sound like bragging, they do not seem to be unique. My friends recount their children's accomplishments with the same wonder and incredulity. One sophisticated, wealthy mom tells blushingly of how, as her son played the piano at high school graduation, she confided proudly to the total stranger beside her, "That's my boy!"

Another friend, normally a model of polite reserve, bellowed across a crowded church the good news that her daughter had been accepted at her first choice of college. Even the cartoon dad in "Hi and Lois" counsels his son, proudly riding on Dad's shoulders after his winning home run, to savor the moment. When the son asks the dad if he's ever had such a Moment, Hi smiles. "Yes," he answers. "It was the proudest moment of my life. Until now."

When parents start telling stories of their kids, they seem blissfully unaware of how boring they've become. The most avid workaholics, the most notorious dragon-ladies in the office turn into charming raconteurs when sharing the new pictures or the latest anecdotes about their offspring.

I listen avidly, delighted that other people freely admit being surpassed by their children. Mine have gone so utterly beyond me that admitting it may cause them to rub it in gleefully. In many ways,

I'm the quintessential nerd: shy, introverted, preferring a novel to a party any day. I bumble when I must think on my feet and blunder through any communication with more than one person at a time. It is not hard to imagine my astonishment, then, when my son is elected president of the student body and my daughter treasurer of the Black Student Union at college. As a colleague once asked, "How could such an introvert have such extroverted kids?" I am not prone to quote the Bible in casual conversation, but I could have answered, "You will do greater works than these."

It strikes me that this line from John's gospel could function as a healthy antidote to the descriptions I've been reading lately about people who function only with negative energy. If there's not a crisis, they don't act. If things are going too calmly, they create emergencies. The simplest things — a burned-out light bulb, a gas tank low on fuel, a deadline at work — become inflated to earth-shaking events. Such exaggeration is the only way these folks get juiced; the writers, artists, and other right-brained folks I hang around with are notorious for working in this mode. I think what I'd like to see my children develop instead is an awareness of how much even our slightest efforts please God. In fact, we don't have to do anything, just be, for God to delight in us. In *Amazing Grace,* Richard Rohr asks the question, "When your daughter keeps running toward you and calling you Daddy, do you really care that much whether she stumbles a few times on the way?"[23]

From a maternal standpoint, I remember the day my son proudly brought home the glass jar of jam he'd made in kindergarten. It gleamed crimson in the sunshine; it probably represented hours of work. As he ran up the front sidewalk, he tripped and fell. The glass shattered; the jam sprayed all over the lawn. I have never loved him more than at that moment, nor felt closer to the heart of God.

On that same sidewalk, Katie came running one wintry day when I had already started the car to drive her (late again) to school. "Telephone!" she yelled as she fell flat on the ice at the gate. My first reaction was frustration: "Why didn't you let the answering machine get it?" Then I realized how hard she was trying to help. Her tights torn, a bump on her forehead, her back aching, tears streaming down her cheeks, she'd seen all her efforts diminished. Gathering her into my arms, I knew then how compassionate God must feel toward those who fail.

Having said all that, I'll return to the subject of accomplishments. How it must please God to see the extraordinary things people do in their ordinary routines. How difficult it must be to sit with the dying, to walk with the prisoner, to study the cells that might hold the cure for disease, to rehearse a line from a play or a symphony for the umpteenth time, to hold in our bodies the tensions created by twentieth-century careers, to balance budgets and stressful commitments, to puzzle through a diagnosis, a nuance, a computer design.

What gets us through? I don't know the answers for everyone, but I know that I'd like my children to think of God smiling, of God delighting in them, of God dancing with intense pleasure just because they're alive. "God delivered me because God delighted in me," says the psalmist (Ps. 18:19). In the same vein, I once heard a shy person describe his efforts to be more outgoing: "I just imagine all the angels doing somersaults of joy," he said. "Then it gets a little easier."

That image seems powerful enough to offset the negative motivations, the misperceptions of a punitive God wielding a giant club. When my children face crises, or even when they struggle to roll out of bed and negotiate another day, I hope they can look into the face of God and find the beaming pride of the Super Citizen's mom.

— 10 —

TWISTING IN THE WIND: THE PARENT-TEACHER CONFERENCE

W HILE PARENTING has its proud moments, it also has its down side, when the fickle mother of the super citizen swears she's never seen the kid before. Our wish to disassociate from our offspring hits its peak at the dreaded parent-teacher conference. There, we wear the glummest faces collected in the high school cafeteria since the mandatory-freshman-parent-orientation. Clearly not folks who want to be here, we fantasize about the twenty-seven places we'd rather be. The demeaning way we are treated reinforces our rock-bottom self-image: herded into the cafeteria with zero privacy, expected to hoist aging, overweight bodies onto picnic table benches opposite people young enough to be our students — who are in fact the faculty, the "wisdom figures" in this bunch. In order to be heard, we shout over each other, revealing to the embarrassed multitudes the excruciatingly private details of our teenagers' grades.

The teenagers themselves acquire alienated stares and rigid postures. In a Frankenstein transformation, the kids we joked with over dinner become defensive and remote, as if their weekend plans involved suicide bombing attacks rather than a movie or basketball game. With studied coolness, they adopt punk slouches, fists plunged into low-riding jeans pockets, eyes shaded by the visors of baseball caps. "Failure" blazes across their foreheads; neon lights shrieking "outcast!" would almost be redundant. Every parent wonders darkly if this is the first step toward a career in serial killing.

Dads who would slap each other's backs at the car wash nod furtively in passing; moms who slogged in tandem through the fundraising committee stare frostily past each other. Recognition implies the kiss of death; the only kindness is pretending not to know each other. After all, only the most miserable wretches attend this ordeal chummily termed "parent-teacher conferences." We wouldn't be here if our kids were on the honor roll. We have (ahem — nervous clearing of throat) failed at our most important task.

The extent of our failure becomes clear only as we make the rounds. One computer printout after another reveals the dismal score: homework not turned in; quizzes flunked; opportunities for extra credit assiduously avoided. The teachers slog caffeine and try to retain the calm, professional courtesy that will prevent us from groveling or sobbing at their feet. Their deliberate avoidance of questions like, "So where were *you* when he spent the night before the final on the phone?" only underscores our painful fall from grace.

The compassion of a few young teachers makes me want to weep. With a concern that could not be faked, the religion teacher asks my son if there's anything he can do to help, to make the class more relevant. Between the two young men stretches a gap that makes the Lazarus-Dives chasm look miniscule. The young theology teacher is everything I'd want my son to be: devoted to his wife and students, living in solidarity with the poor, committed to bringing the finest contemporary theologians into his classroom. He must try desperately to communicate with kids who visit from another planet. As he tries to guide them toward the examined life, they gravitate toward rugby, fast cars, and throbbing sound systems. While the teacher tries intently to reach my son, I wonder vaguely which lurid, beer-sloganed T-shirt my offspring has chosen for the occasion.

I toy with various lame excuses. Wonder if he's heard this one: "Heh-heh; he's fifteen years old"? On the torture bench, I remember how a colleague's fourteen-year-old discovered the perfect button to push with his dad, the respected chair of a college English department. Semester after semester, this dedicated professional would drag himself to grueling conferences about his son, wickedly devoted to flunking English. Ah, they do know how to get our elderly goats, pinioned here on the hot seats!

Trapped in this picnic-bench cage, I try desperately to concoct conversational ploys. "Well, they'll grow out of it" doesn't seem to cut it for football quarterbacks who lurch besides doll-sized moms. The only decent solution seems to be to admit one's abysmal sin in this public confessional and genuflect abjectly before the teacher with profuse apologies and firm promises of amendment. Then exit as gracefully as possible, saving for the parking lot the sanctions upon the son who's lassoed us into this predicament.

As usual, the understandings don't seem to come until sufficient time, that gracious restorer of perspective, has elapsed. In this case, we're talking lots of time spread over four children. The sad truth is that for folks supposedly in the know, professional teachers and writers, we have a dismal history of faithful attendance at conferences for the parenting-impaired. Yup, we know the latest educational trends; we read the journals; we attend the conventions and keep up the credentials. But somehow we can't hold a candle to the wonderful janitor down the block whose kid gets straight As and a full ride through college. Our frequent trips through cafeteria-table hell are tributes to God's sense of humor and our increasing sense of humility.

But maybe such front-row intimacy with dire report cards offers a chance to recoup low self-esteem by salvaging some insight from the occasion. In exploring God with children, I've discovered repeatedly how the weirdest events of a parent's day can bring blessing. The word "blessing" may be a stretch, but it's used in good company. Mitch and Kathy Finley, nationally respected experts on family life, recently returned home after giving a highly acclaimed workshop on parenting. The welcoming scene created by their three teenagers wasn't pretty — extending even to the wide-open front door with one son's key dangling from the lock. "The blessing was that no one was home," Kathy laughs in retrospect. "If they had been, we would have killed them!"

When, after several days, my sense of humor is restored, I remember a conference when the fifth-grade teacher described my older son. "Tends to be a little spacey. Gets so absorbed in his reading, he doesn't realize we've started the spelling test!"

"How perceptive of you," I'd murmured, wondering why it all sounded so familiar. Then I realized she'd been right on target, describing not only my son but also my father. Dad is a brilliant professor emeritus of English, whose students remember him twenty-five years later for love of literature and warm humor. He is also a man who moves in a world of ideas; mundane matters like scheduling are unwelcome intrusions. Fortunately, in the academic world, most of the details can be handled by competent secretaries. Then Dad can return to the company of literary heroes, where he walks with grace and joy.

While parents expect to find something of themselves in their offspring, they are often startled to discover a previous generation there. When my older son challenged the principal on a false charge of misbehavior, it echoed an event a half century before. When Dad's baseball team was being punished, prevented from playing a big game, he sidled up to the teacher and whispered, "To err is human; to forgive, divine." The team, forgiven, played.

I suppose my grandmother fretted over the report card as I did, our future-vision severely restricted to the here and now. Little did she suspect that her spacey son would grow up to be a spacey professor, with an equally spacey grandson. My reluctant conference attendance has given me a solidarity not only with other limited human beings, but also with generations before.

But most important of all, this insidious form of torture gives me a glimpse into a quality of Jesus that I call "sad tiredness." It surfaces repeatedly as disciple after disciple demonstrates how sweepingly they have misunderstood him. That catch in his voice, that hesitation in his heart rings familiar to the survivor of the cafeteria conference. We hear it when James and John request thrones on his right and left. It echoes again when Peter warns him blatantly that talk about justice will get him in trouble. Philip seems to be a perpetual teenager who asks the perennial stupid question. Jesus addresses him with parental weariness, "Have I been with you all this time, Philip, and you still do not know me?" (John 14:9). As the disciples jostle for favors, wish audibly for the perks, and theorize about their power in the kingdom, we can almost hear Jesus whisper, "How could you have gotten it so wrong?"

To the arrogant teenager we long to say, "Everything I value I've tried to pass on to you, and you have set it aside." The same perplexity echoes through the scriptural story of the unfruitful vineyard. It details all the gifts God has carefully provided to nurture a vineyard, which in turn produces only wild grapes. With all natural expectations dashed, God asks the unanswerable question: "What more was there to do for my vineyard that I have not done in it?" (Isa. 5:4). We have not been the perfect parents, but when our children disappoint us, we begin to understand how our own failures must sadden God.

Yet the stunning mystery quivering at the heart of all this is that despite the disappointment or even the broken heart, we continue to love the errant child. At the moment we are closest to strangling him or her, we would also hurl our bodies in front of anyone who threatened that precious life. We may bemoan the terrible study habits, the blithe disregard for an education that is costing us a fortune — but God help anyone else who criticizes! Deep down, we love that child with an aching ferocity. We value that life more than our own. In the paradox, we glimpse a God heartbroken over our inadequacies yet, at the same time, sending the most precious Son to redeem us. Until I had children, I could never hold such polarities in tension; the two ideas could not coexist in my mind. Now I see how what I despair of most completely is also what I most deeply cherish.

Biblically, it's a common thread, where parents and God and sons seem to take interchangeable roles. As the parable father peers far down the dusty road, yearning for the son who squandered the inheritance, the stance is familiar. It isn't the rabbi who welcomes the son home, just as it isn't his apostles, but his mother who prompts Jesus' first miracle. Only the parent/child relationship, it seems, is woven close enough to bear the weight of the ultimate truths. Familiarity may breed contempt, but the round contours and smoothed edges of home also create a relaxed state where the guard is down and the understanding can occur. A cluster of similar biblical stories resonates with a message learned better in the household than in the temple: don't waste energy on the mistake, the grade, the failure; celebrate instead the son come home.

When he doesn't, the tragedy is fierce. Perhaps a story told in 2 Samuel should be required reading for all parents. King David's son Absalom murders another beloved son, usurps the throne, and leads an army against David. Yet the only news from the battle David wants to hear is contained in a question he repeats to the messenger, "Is it well with the young man Absalom?" When he hears of Absalom's death, a victory that restores his own power, he is devastated. David weeps, "Absalom, my son, my son Absalom! Would I had died instead of you, O Absalom, my son, my son!" The cry of anguish could echo through our secondary schools and colleges, our battlefields, our AIDS treatment centers, our neighborhoods ripped by gang violence.

For David as for any parent, what matters is not the betrayal, but the life of the beloved child. Only through such a paradox can we understand that no matter how heinous the offense, God the father still holds us dear. Most parents probably wonder at times why they got themselves into such an uncomfortable role. Adolescence seems to force the issue: What's become of the infant sleeping sweetly under the bunny soft blanket?

Maybe that's a good time to remember the reconciliations of the early years. One day, totally absorbed in writing, I forgot to fetch a child from school. Twenty minutes late, I found him standing forlornly on the corner. Guilt-ridden, I rushed into my frantic apology: "I got so deep into an article, I forgot to check the clock!" With a lopsided smile, he answered, "I know. Same thing happens to me when I'm reading."

Once when we all had strep, I discovered miserably that children get huge, horrendous shots. Each child, waiting a turn, hears the yelp of the one before, as the long needle of penicillin pierces the hip. It typifies life's injustices to small people when the adult wimps get no shots, only pills. With heart and throat both sore, I started to cry on the way home from the doctor's office, tears splashing the steering wheel. Then an equally tear-streaked child offered me her plastic ring, a pediatrician's reward for good behavior. Even in her hurt, she reached out to comfort me. Whenever I hear about the mercy of God, I'll remember that gift. People lucky enough to have forgiving children can believe in a forgiving God.

Conference time is also prime time to recall our own offenses. Only through those did we ourselves learn how God, greater than any hurt, can forgive any wrong. Seared into my psyche is an image from Catholic grade school. Every day as we filed into that brick building, we'd pass a statue of the Sacred Heart, his arms outstretched. At the time I didn't fully appreciate that wide and welcoming embrace. But now that I know how badly I can err, I turn to a God who speaks through that image: "Did I mention that I love you? *This* much? No matter what?"

Back in grade school, long before parenthood, I couldn't understand why a God as great as ours is purported to be could love a creature so prone to failure as myself. Parenthood provided an insider's look at that question.

Didn't I fall in love, hopelessly, immediately, and forever, with a tiny being still streaked with blood, whose birth had caused me considerable pain and whose presence promised to interrupt my sleep and drain my bank account for years ahead? Was God's loving me any more logical? As Thomas More explains to his son-in-law William Roper in the film *A Man for All Seasons,* "Finally, it's not a matter for reason. Finally it's a matter of love."

Should we have any doubt about the forgiveness of God, we need only look into the face of Jesus. The story of the woman caught in adultery (John 8:1–11) stands out, not only for the nonjudgmental way Jesus treats her, but for his attitude toward her accusers. The Pharisees have attacked her viciously. Yet he responds to them nonviolently even after they embarrass and humiliate her publicly.

My children's faces are open and fresh. I dread their ever becoming angry, pickle faces, poisoned by buried resentments. So they need to learn how good people express anger, resolve conflicts, ask for the grace to forgive, and work to reconcile. In these efforts, they will catch a hint of God's forgiveness. And I will learn to endure the parent-teacher conferences, a powerful learning experience. There we know that we are like God when we give our hearts into such small hands, then live out a commitment which can carry a staggering cost.

— *11* —

THE SAGA OF
THE PINK SUIT

P ARENTS WHO GO from awards ceremony to teacher conference may think that a roller coaster describes their experience better than a boat launching. Sometimes both extremes meet at once: a dentist appointment, a rare grace. The two come together in this saga....

It was outrageously expensive and wildly impractical. Even the most sympathetic male would find it hard to understand why I coveted it. The pink suit also fit like a glove and was stunningly beautiful. My older daughter, Colleen, and I stumbled upon it during one of our shopping trips meant to find her a swimsuit or a pair of jeans. Inevitably, when we set out with such a definite daughter agenda, we wound up finding treasures for Mom.

Graciously, Colleen would then assume the role of fashion consultant, giving me a critical reading on every garment I tried. One look at her face told me if a new outfit rated further consideration. Her eyes lit up when I tried on the pink suit. But after long consideration of the price, the necessity of dry cleaning, the limited number of occasions on which I could wear it, we decided to return it (reluctantly) to the rack and concentrate on more practical purchases.

Of course the saga does not end there. The following day, I was scheduled for a dental appointment so grueling that the dentist had prescribed Valium in advance. That ruled out my driving and placed my daughter in the inverted role of "taking Mommy to the dentist." She came through like a champion: pleading for more drugs when the painkillers had no effect, holding my hand for shots, trying to relax me with soothing talk of languid beach vacations.

Despite Colleen's efforts, the anesthesia that would have knocked out a three-hundred-pound man failed to have the desired effect, and the dentist swore she'd go to jail if she increased the dosage. I would, it developed, be facing the drill cold turkey.

One look at the sharp needles and menacing instruments hidden behind me made Colleen desperate. In a daring ploy to distract me, she bribed: "What reward would you like after it's all over?" My rational faculty blurred by the drugs, I seized the chance with childish greed: "the pink suit!"

Four hours later, with a tooth that felt like a pumpkin, a system full of drugs, a head full of fuzz, and a mouth full of pain, I collapsed into bed. There on the pillow was a classy shopping bag from a posh department store. Even in my woozy condition, I didn't need to look inside. Curled in tissue paper, there lay the pink suit in the perfect size, every child's most outlandish Christmas wish come true.

One might logically ask what such a story has to do with theology. Maybe nothing. Maybe it's simply a tale of feminine vanity, a frivolous story that would baffle many people.

Or, maybe everything. Perhaps the pink suit is a vehicle that tells us something of God, just as more traditional symbols like candle and loaf, chalice and vine call up another reality, awaken another level of meaning. For one thing, it says that a child, taken to the dentist for many years, with hand held empathetically and the promise of a frozen yogurt afterward, knows how to return the favor when her turn comes. If someone has been the beneficiary of enough trip-to-the-dentist compassion, she knows how to reciprocate.

Wasn't the modeling dimension crucial to the message of Jesus? The theme "Go and do likewise" threads its way through many of his stories. The tales of the early church show a community gradually learning to act as he did: by trial and error, praying together, touching, healing, feeding, expelling demons in every guise.

Another element of this saga is the same clothing metaphor that runs throughout Scripture. Isaiah writes:

> I will greatly rejoice in the Lord...
> for he has clothed me with the garments of salvation,
> he has covered me with the robe of righteousness,
> as a bridegroom decks himself with a garland,
> and as a bride adorns herself with her jewels. (61:10)

Speaking of the vindication of the Israelites, God promises: "You shall be a crown of beauty in the hand of the Lord, and a royal diadem in the hand of your God" (Isa. 62:3). Finally, God says with loving mercy to the people: "Put on your beautiful garments, O Jerusalem, the holy city" (Isa. 52:1).

We usually associate ancient Hebrew society with harsh poverty. Yet these passages overflow with abundance. When it comes to the royal crowns of God's children, no one counts the cost. It's quite possible the writers were using hyperbole, praising God's bounty with an extravagance well beyond their usual grim ration. How astonishing, they seem to say, that we who usually wear the scratchy, ill-fitting garment are in some sense clothed with the grace of the deity, the lavish wardrobe of King Solomon or the Queen of Sheba.

In the New Testament, the metaphor takes on another spin: we are to clothe ourselves in Christ (Rom. 13:14; Gal. 3:27). The "great portent" in Revelation is "a woman clothed with the sun, . . . and on her head a crown of twelve stars" (12:1). The bride of the Lamb, or the beloved of God, is "clothed with fine linen, bright and pure" (Rev. 19:8).

For someone to make such imaginative leaps from the ordinary requires a jumping-off place, some foretaste, some glimpse of the shimmering satin. To then appropriate the image to oneself, one must have a deeply rooted sense of what all humans justly deserve: the natural dignity that befits every son or daughter of God. The appearance is deceptive, says such a stance. We may not be costumed for the part, but beneath the misleading surface, we are indeed the children of the most high king.

It's fascinating to observe how some people are at home in the most awkward circumstances, while others writhe with little apparent provocation. In the worst conditions of the concentration camps, some people forgot their own suffering to care for others; some people descended to the same bestial level as their Nazi jailers. By a mysterious alchemy, the first group transformed their prison attire to majestic garments of compassion. They became blessing and balm for each other.

In less dramatic circumstances, I've observed the teenagers who hang around our home. They may all wear identical jeans and T-shirts. The older ones enjoy a kegger; the younger adolescents seem incapable of independent action and travel together in packs. But it is almost always possible to differentiate one or two by virtue of their unusual courtesy: disentangling himself from a huddle of peers, a teenaged boy will greet the Great Ostracized class of parents, offer to help with the dishes, and even grab a broom if necessary. Sometimes one girl in a group will stand out not so much for her beauty (most kids, because of their youth, have a certain amount of that), but for a presence, a sense of self that is assertive without being abrasive, confident without being arrogant.

They are not perfect kids, but I suspect their parents instilled in them some tough fiber that will withstand the pressure to abuse drugs, alcohol, and sex. They may not be the straight-A students, but they have something more precious: a clarity about who they are, a deep conviction that they are precious to someone. Meister Eckhart describes our identity: "The seed of God is in us. Now the seed of a pear tree grows into a pear tree; and a hazel seed grows into a hazel tree; a seed of God grows into God."[24]

Perhaps it is a far reach from seeds to pink suits. But even pampered people in modern homes need a glimmer of grace, a reminder of our high calling. We need our diamond from the king's crown, even if it's only a drop of dew on a pansy's velvet surface or the costume jewelry inherited from a beloved relative. We may be surrounded by material comforts, but still we seem to need frequent reminders of who we are.

As if to prove that theory, I regularly endure a moment of panic before every public speaking engagement. About five minutes before I'm slated to go on stage, I blank on content, lose any concept of why I'm doing this, and wonder how fast I can find the nearest exit. At that time, I usually vanish into the lady's room for a few deep breaths and the kind of urgent prayer that drowning people must say as the waters fill their lungs. Then I emerge from the rest room with confidence restored and energy renewed. "Bring on the audience!" I want to shout, lunging toward the podium.

For the next few speeches, I have a new weapon in the preparation arsenal. I'll enter the lady's room and look in the mirror. It will gleam back at me in stunning pink: wildly impractical, outrageously expensive. I will stroke its soft skirt and remember a day at the dentist, a little girl who once put in her time in the dentist's chair too, and a mature girl's thoughtfulness that every parent deserves at least once. The audience will not know the saga, nor guess that something pink's at play. But perhaps with enthusiasm and conviction, I can remind them that they too are bejeweled; they too are children of the king who clothes them in luxury and extravagance, who attaches no price and no strings to the gifts showered on beloved children.

— *12* —

GOD OF THE (AAUGH!)
DRIVING LESSON

A NYONE WHO SURVIVES the dentist's drill should be able to pass this acid test. As I sit terrified in a car crammed with fifteen-year-old boys, my own at the wheel, I wonder, "Where is God *now?*" Rush-hour traffic bolts feverishly, my stomach wrenches, my neck stiffens, rigid with tension. Acid rock on the radio fills the car with whining, shrieking dissonance. If Dante had had a teenaged driver, he surely would've added this trip to his circles of hell.

All around me, solitary business types in somber suits are commuting to work. In the crystalline stillness of their cars, they probably plan the day's projects and compose themselves serenely for the office. What devilish punishment has consigned me to going the opposite way, an hour round trip *away* from my office? Worse, what has reduced me to such quivering stress that I will arrive there needing Valium, before any work crises have had a chance to develop? The answer is contained in my barely intelligible mutter to the concerned receptionist when I arrive, "I have a teenaged driver."

Surely those five magic words, mumbled at death's door, will compensate abundantly for all the evils I've ever committed. St. Peter (whose teenager probably careened in a mean chariot or raced the fishing boat against Andrew's kid) will embrace me sympathetically and whisk me right past purgatory. "Ah, yes, dear. We understand," he'll cluck soothingly. The angels will gather in empathy and stroke my contorted spine with feathery tenderness. The martyrs will recognize one of their own, a bold, kindred spirit who risked the freeway at 8:00 a.m. As cherubim inquire about the newcomer, they'll nod knowingly and pull out a special throne: deep and cushiony, on heaven's highest porch, with a sweeping view of spectacular sunsets and a steady stream of mai tais — yeah, with little paper umbrellas!

Forgive the fantasizing, but one needs some carrot to endure these rides through terror. Oddly enough, traveling beside a fifteen-year-old boy with a new driver's permit doesn't get much play in classic works on spirituality. Most of those volumes — and I'm the first to find them immensely helpful — seem to have been composed in the hush of a retreat house or the ordered silence of a monastery. Not much help when I'm desperately in need of some soothing to offset the relentless drumming of the rock band....

Even Richard Rohr, whom I suspect may be the St. Francis of our century, gasps, "One day I did five loads of laundry!" He explains that a family visited him and their three children got sick on everything: the sheets, the curtains, etc. Rohr then develops some fine insights on the virtues of parenting, but I get stuck on the sweet innocence of his experience. I long to say, "Excuse me, Father — I've done five loads of laundry almost every day for the last twenty-two years.... Probably more in the predisposable days, when two under two wore diapers."

But one-upmanship is not the point. Perhaps the problem is that during the intensive child-rearing years, parents are too deeply sunk in the experience to have a moment to analyze or appreciate it. Even the Ignatian "examen," a wonderful way of finding God's presence in the day as it ends, inevitably cues me to zonk asleep, exhausted. So the experience of parents, with a few marvelous exceptions like Dolores Curran, Kathleen Chesto, David Thomas, and Pat Livingston, remains largely unmined. It's up to us to figure it out, I guess.

"Aaugh!" I think as horns blare and cars swerve within inches of the unexperienced driver beside me. "Not only do I have to *endure* this; I have to find some *meaning* in it?"

Then my writing and speaking come back to haunt me. "You said God is everywhere — has God abandoned the freeway?" "You said God is constantly present — can pimply companions and throbbing electric guitars drive that presence away?" "You want your children to be able to call on Christ anywhere, at any time — does he not cover you with compassion, even here, even now?" The scriptural one-liner jabs with the worst ferocity: "Who can separate us from the love of Christ?"

So it's either recant all I've written, like some theologian under the torture of the Inquisition, or in desperation reach for the God of rush hour. Searching from that stance does not lessen the panic with which I clutch the armrest or the sharpness with which I draw a shocked breath. It does, however, attune me to the little cues of the Presence. This is, after all, my third teenager, my third trip through highway hell, the third time I've cowered in the passenger seat beside the new driver. In better moments, I realize that "this too will pass."

In fact, I've been weak-kneed with gratitude to my older son, who at twenty-two drives the family fearlessly on mountain roads, through blizzards that would leave me paralyzed with anxiety. I prod myself mercilessly, that would have been impossible had I not, six years ago, endured the days of *his* driver's permit. How convenient it's been for my older daughter to drive her younger sister to day camp, or me to the airport. Again, impossible without the white knuckle days.... Are you showing me something here, dear God, about the rich passage of time and the long lens of eternity?

Certainly time spent in cars with our children isn't a novelty. As one mother sighed, "We just moved to a beautiful new home, but it doesn't really matter. We live in the car." Perhaps one problem with the permit is that parents have worn the chauffeur's cap so long, this burst of independence marks the end of a chapter. Over the years, car-time conversations have offered a window on children's development. Only in Norman Rockwell do kids share intimacies around the hearth. In real life, children's dramatic pronouncements filter from the passenger seat. I still remember an excited seven-year-old clambering into the car.

"Guess what, Mom? I got the role of Mary in the Christmas pageant!"

"Great, honey!"

"But the teacher said if I don't have the costume by tomorrow for dress rehearsal, she'll give the part to Alice!"

For those addicted to happy endings, Mom did what any other liberated, assertive, twentieth-century mother would do: she crumbled. Setting aside the fifty final exams she was supposed to grade that night, she stuffed blue fabric through a sewing machine at midnight. St. Augustine was right: "It is one thing to see the land of peace from a wooded ridge... and another to tread the road that leads to it."

Treading that rocky road, I must acknowledge one benefit: a cozy companionship I might not otherwise have shared in children's tumultuous teenaged years. Seizing the wheel like a trophy, Sean grins and asks facetiously: "You wouldn't want to miss this special bonding time, would you?" Even a rare courtesy kindles, as a small voice from the back seat, like the tenth leper, pipes up politely, "Thank you for driving with us, Mrs. Coffey." I do get an earful of high school gossip, an empathy with their excruciating social codes, a tickle of their humor, and a feel for their musical tastes. If nothing else, this daily jolt of reality will prevent me from getting airy or pious!

It seems to be God's style to push us beyond the surface events. Even when paralyzed with fright, I relish the small, mysterious smile that plays around Sean's mouth when he is driving. He's pretty good at this new skill, I'll concede. I recognize that familiar hint of smile from watching anyone absorbed in what they do well: my friend who's a potter, my son's friend who skis as if it were ballet, a teacher who entertains a class with relaxed good humor, my own delight when I get a line in a new poem right.

In the absence of rituals marking puberty, our society confers a driver's license. So Sean pivots on a threshold, and while a brass choir isn't playing a triumphant entrance, we're poised in a liminal space. Tentatively, with plenty of joking to cover the tension, he is seizing his own life, the adulthood that hovers just around the corner. Sure, there will be some scrapes along the way, some speeding tickets and some nearly averted crashes. But faith tells me, even as I twist with anxiety, that grace will carry the day, that he will arrive at maturity, and in the future I'll be grateful when he can pick me up from work as my car gets repaired. Yes, some parents endure terrible tragedies and discover their children's bodies in twisted wreckage. My heart aches for them. But the vast majority survive adolescence, just as they sidetracked the dangerous pitfalls of toddlerhood. That statistic alone must prove the existence of guardian angels.

Maybe it's pushing the analogy, but some unseen companion has always been at my side through the roller coasters of my own experience. Unsure and tentative as I've launched new adventures, I've counted on that affirmation, that "you can do it!" message. If I don't want my children to remain forever dependent, I must pay the price to guide them into the paths of self-reliance. It may sound a bit forced, but as Sean reaches school and grudgingly hands the car keys back to me, I choke out, "Good job, Hon!" What's a little hypocrisy among family members?

Then comes the moment when grace rushes in. Despite all my efforts to bring God into the car pool, I love the moment when it empties. With the car all to myself, I dial the radio to the soft liquid of classical music. I reclaim my thoughts — and my wheel. "Heh, heh," I chortle, crazed with power. "*I'm* in the driver's seat!" It's an exhilaration that the childless never sense as they slip blithely behind the wheels of their cars. Poor folks — they're always in charge. They miss the joyful ebb and flow of surrendering control and regaining it. Nor will they ever celebrate a safe arrival with the heartfelt gratitude of the licensed driver who sits beside the driver's permit. Whenever I see a picture of the pope deplaning and kissing the ground of a foreign country, I think, "Yup, that's the relief I feel." If it weren't so grubby, I might start kissing the floor of my garage.

— *13* —

"PETER AND THE WOLF"

IT MAY BE A STRETCH from the highway to the concert hall, but people alert to God's surprise appearances can encounter that presence in both places. My children and I draw fine insights from "Peter and the Wolf."

Sliding into our seats in the symphony hall, I admire again its rich wood textures, its tremor of anticipation as the musicians tune up, its liminal aura of beauty about to be born. We gather on a threshold here, and the children, dressed in their best, are poised with excitement. Beside me, Katie strokes her new purple skirt of some impractical, flimsy fabric like satin, and I quit fretting about how to wash it. Some things are good for the soul, and every time she twirls, I share her joy in the swishing pirouette.

As the concert begins, I remember a retreat which focused on beauty as the door to the sacred. The day became a banquet for the senses as we smelled fragrant ointment, touched marble sculpture, admired sunset over the mountain range, and listened to music.

The retreat director, an accomplished musical composer, has a keen ear for beauty himself. He explains that the aesthetic dimension of religion calls us to drink of the holy and live in the place of real peace. When Jesus came to us as the Christ, the anointed one, it wasn't as if he identified himself as "Jesus Jones." He came with the healing of balm and the fragrance of perfume.

Returning home rich with these insights, I wonder how to translate them to my children. It's a complex question, so I tackle it with logic. We become what we gaze on. Therefore, if our thirst for beauty is satisfied, peace and joy wells within us. If we are deprived, we become depressed or violent. It seems then as if I should replenish the simmering potpourri pot, play soft classical music, and fill the house with flowers. That is probably an oversimplification, but it's a start.

The next step is ordering tickets for "Peter and the Wolf." We owe our presence at this concert to the retreat director. As he played the tape, he mimed for us the victorious procession at the concert's end. Retreatants relished the unique sight of a priest with a doctorate pretending to be Peter. He stood tall, puffed up in triumph as he pretended to drag the wolf by the tail.

Of course, it's more than the simple story of boy snares wild animal. Symbols always have wider implications: the routing of depression, the valiant person conquering inertia, the courage of those resisting oppression. In the triumphant procession, I can imagine Sojourner Truth, Dorothy Day, Archbishop Romero and all the martyrs of El Salvador, Rigoberta Menchú Tum, Thea Bowman, Catherine of Siena, Martin Luther King Jr., Edith Stein, Thomas Merton, Aung San Suu Kyi, Rosa Parks.

Even incomplete, it's a stunning litany of heroes, an inspiring company of saints. But what compels me to buy the tickets is the priest saying softly, "If I had a child, I would take my child to 'Peter and the Wolf.'" His remark is at once poignant and persuasive. If anyone in the world would make a fine father, it is he. Of all the wistful ironies in the world, he is childless. But I have the chance, and probably a longer-winded rationale for my presence at this concert than anyone else here!

Unfortunately, it turns out to be the P.C. version, where evil is declawed, the duck is only hiding and not munched, the wolf isn't killed but released to the wilderness in a burst of environmental awareness. Sigh. I hope the children still get the point.

Peter was fine as he strutted his stuff, and I suppose that's what I wanted Katie to see. We can tackle whatever challenge, enter whatever battle life sends, and love the process. Conflict is an opportunity to sharpen our skills, broaden our creativity, and hone our talents. Confronting death, Terry Williams wrote in *Refuge,* "One begins to almost trust the intruder as a presence that demands greater intent toward life."[25]

Can I tell all that to a ten-year-old? Of course not. But I can plant seeds: embedding the story deep in children's psyches, whistling the theme at appropriate moments, trying to connect my children's personal struggles with other human conflicts, giving their efforts meaning by placing them within this larger context.

I also challenge my children to heroism. A colleague once complained, "The trouble with a fat culture is that kids aren't often called to be heroes." Knowing she was probably right, I was delighted to discover the emphasis many high schools now place on service projects.

For a while, they set aside the competition for college and spend time on activities that don't "compute." Service projects are serious, but their value is intangible; they provide to sheltered adolescents a view of another world and another view of themselves. If they were once content to be the pampered darlings, they mature quickly, their gifts called forth by a needy world. There children die, beautiful faces are horribly mutilated, and grave problems have no quick-fix solutions.

Teenagers can bring youthful energy to places where enthusiasm has dwindled and people have borne the burden of suffering too long. Champion swimmers adjust their strokes to those of children with cerebral palsy. Hulking quarterbacks, following the skilled movements of gnarled hands, learn to crochet. The National Merit scholarship winner tutors an illiterate grandmother. Awkward high school students feed Jell-O to AIDS patients. Playing checkers with the burn victims at Children's Hospital, adolescents wipe tears on the sleeves of their sweaters. Bending over to offer a milkshake to a woman with osteoporosis, they seem to grow a notch taller.

The intensive care waiting room may have been foreign territory to the children of the happy-ending Disney era, but in the human journey, we are always passing from the familiar to the unfamiliar. What keeps us going is our images of hope. Perhaps one of the most persistent is a triumphant Peter, dragging a wolf by the tail.

— *14* —

SOMETHING SOLID,
LIKE A TURRET

THE GRACE AND DIGNITY of the concert hall can also be found within the granite walls of a castle, the past echoing into the present. Perhaps that perpetual human thirst for beauty helps explain why people raised in a democracy, who've never lived in a monarchy, are nevertheless fascinated by royalty. The first fairy tales we hear must plant the images of kings and queens, castles and crowns. It's a romantic world where "noblesse oblige," the dragons are eventually (albeit messily) slain, and the day ends with a proper ball. Music fills the great hall, the brocades shimmer in soft candlelight, and the knights bow courteously before their ladies.

Perhaps it is a safety valve for the psyche to imagine this royal retreat. When the crass advertising and the neon signs and the french-fried slogans have hammered our aesthetic sensibilities to pulp, we can still flee to the image of Camelot where courtly love flourishes, "the snow may never slosh upon the hillside," and the nobility lift finely wrought chalices of hammered gold to each other's lips.

Poetic as it seems, this is not simply the fantasizing of Camelot-besotted old people. The evidence suggests that the British aren't the only ones who reverence the ideal, if not the reality, of royalty. From the popularity of Renaissance festivals in various locales around the country, I suspect that many people long for a nobler way of life, removed from used car dealers and shrieking gimmicks to sell hamburgers.

A similar trend is refurbishing Victorian palaces and mansions as bed-and-breakfast retreats. A friend recalled her stay in one: "I had my own turret. That made it ever so much easier to carry on the duties of my queendom!" Tourists still flock to San Simeon, the Hearst castle in California, and its clones around the country. Through a leap of the imagination, we want to associate, if only briefly, with the days of the discreet servants, the wagonloads of fresh flowers delivered for every room, the roaring bonfire in the stone fireplace. Give us something solid, the psyche seems to say. We're tired of plastic impermanence and planned obsolescence. Take us back to builders who designed a casement to last a thousand years.

Perhaps we also need this potent reminder, encased in brick, that we too are builders, engaged in tasks that will outlive us. The architects of medieval castles and cathedrals knew that they would probably not live to see their work completed. Yet people with a variety of skills contributed their masonry, stained glass, or wood carving, knowing that the next generation would continue the construction. Those soaring spires and glowing windows are their gift to us, across the centuries. While we and our children may not be building Buckingham Palace or Chartres cathedral, we are nonetheless building our lives, our happiness, as co-creators with God. When it seems that the stakes are small or the stage narrow, parents would be wise to adapt and follow the advice often given teachers: "We affect eternity. We never know where our influence stops."

As usual, it takes lived experience to thoroughly convince me of this deeply rooted yearning. I recently attended a Renaissance wedding, where bride and groom wore crowns, the attendants wore medieval attire, including swords buckled onto the lords, and a juggler entertained the guests with the traditional patter of the "wise fool." My youngest daughter happily entered the fantasy world, donning one of my slightly altered bridesmaid dresses with a swishing train and a hennin, the cone-shaped headdress with trailing chiffon. For the duration of the day, we addressed her with high courtesy by her middle name, "Lady Margaret." She responded in kind, bowing with dignity to her loyal subjects.

Several weeks later, I became "Queen for a Day" when I had the chance to stay in the castle, now a conference center, built by General William Palmer, the railroad magnate. He had a keen sense of place when he erected Glen Eyrie in the Garden of the Gods near Colorado Springs. The sturdy stones of the architecture echo the red rock formations of the setting. Castle turrets and rock spires nudge a cobalt sky; both nature and building fit a grand scale. Crossing the drawbridge over emerald lawns where columbine and pansies color the flower beds, one enters another era.

Descending the grand staircase, brushing the carved wooden balustrade, one feels transformed, as if the setting lends the human residents some of its dignity. In these gracious surroundings, it is easier to believe my life is not little. The high ceilings, the carved wooden rafters, the French windows overlooking the courtyard, the fountains spilling over with liquid light reaffirm that human beings should be housed in buildings that respect their inherent dignity.

I know: people live in miserable shacks beneath leaking tin roofs. We are rightly appalled by such misery because it contradicts our belief in every person's right to adequate shelter. We abhor the gap between peoples and work toward the goal of fitting dwellings for all the world's children.

The castle represents the ideal: the creweled chairs beside the fireplace reinforce human dignity. In a palatial setting, one should sip only the finest sherry, read only the classics, have only the most exalted conversations. Of course that doesn't happen: rich people exchange banalities no matter how lovely their surroundings. Beneath the surface beauty linger the questions and doubts.

In the face of such ambivalence, I looked to children for an honest reading on our palatial digs. One three-year-old surveyed the stained-glass windows and whispered, "Get your princess dress on, Mommy!" All the children in our group threw their energies into discovering secret passageways and exploring hidden nooks. They scrambled up steps and over balconies, checked out every slit in every wall. Perhaps they were delighted with architecture that suggested and shadowed, in contrast to sterile apartment buildings where residents fight to preserve their individuality in uniform cubicles.

With typical mischief, I'd hinted that the children had better keep their swords handy in case a dragon lurked beneath the drawbridge. The older ones dismissed my fantasy, but the eyes of Dan, the youngest boy, grew wide. When a tour guide told us the story of grease bins from the kitchen, left outside, being overturned during the night, she niftily omitted her suspicion that bears had been the sloppy visitors. Instead she alluded to mammoth footprints climbing back up the mountain. Dan's voice was hardly bigger than a breath as he surmised, "It must've been a small dragon...."

"Ahh!" I thought. "A new recruit for Camelot!" How important it is to feed the imagination with story and nourish the spirit with objects of beauty and permanence. Precious little in our lives is lasting, and many children cope with ongoing change in their primary relationships. Of course it won't solve all society's ills, but don't myth and possibility help small children stand taller? Isn't that one reason we tell our children the story of David and Goliath?

The realist intrudes with a practical question. All very nice, but what's the message here for the great majority of us who don't live in palaces? We consider ourselves lucky to glimpse a little beauty or snatch a moment of quiet in our ordinary day. How accessible is this royalty stuff to most folks?

As close as the nearest library, one might answer. The child who can walk freely through the world of fairy tales and legends has an inner armor, a psychic defense against the petty and trivial. The child who has vicariously hob-nobbed with knights and ladies knows that the same potential for nobility resides within him or herself.

Another answer might be, as close as the natural world. The natural elements widely used in castle building alert us to the more easily accessible palace of nature. If we look hard enough, we can find echoes in the jewels of lakes, the shimmering brocades of meadows, the arches of tall trees, the sturdy anchors of boulders, the crewel embroidery of wildflowers, the banquet of vegetables and fruits. Perhaps it takes a Francis of Assisi to compose the Canticle to the Sun, but we can all learn from him to call the moon our sister and the wind our brother.

Today, a beautiful, ordered home is almost impossible without a flock of servants to maintain it. Yet children follow their instincts to create their own castles, even if it's a hiding place under the pine tree or a tent beneath the kitchen table. Their yearning for lofty space and secret contours may also explain children's messy, hard-for-moms-to-understand habit of collecting: rocks, shells, bits of wood. Are these collections, annoying to the house cleaner, some silent attempts to grasp the larger, natural world, to hold some bit of its wonder closer to ourselves?

Suspecting a "yes" answer to that question, I now regret the money spent on plastic gimmicks for my children. I remember more positively the times we spent time and money to get in touch with God's creation: a trip to the botanic gardens instead of a movie, a weekend in the mountains for a birthday gift, a Christmas holiday spent skiing instead of buying trinkets. I am grateful for the rich, evocative experiences they have had, like sitting on a back porch in Missouri hearing my aunts and uncles tell stories, for meals they've shared with several generations, for the hush that falls with the first snowfall of the season.

Whenever I've squandered time and energy on something that is beneath me, I remember an incident that occurred frequently while I was nursing my children. All our babies were addicted to the pacifier: a fact I regretted when, eight months pregnant with no. 4, I crawled under the crib of no. 3 in the middle of the night. He howled in outrage at losing his sucker. I wondered if I'd find it before getting stuck like Pooh in Rabbit's front door.

As feeding time approached, the babies would chomp furiously on their pacifiers. But when I'd try to pull out the pacifier (with the mighty WHUMP! of its suction), they'd scream like doomed souls. The source of genuine nurture was close by, but they flailed around wretchedly, hunting for the plastic substitute. How often we turn from the generous outpouring of a prolific God and twist ourselves into knots over much lesser problems. We complain myopically, missing the graces showered on us daily. We act like children nervously ransacking the cupboards for food, ignoring a prodigious banquet.

Good theology has the same uplifting tone of abundance. Rather than demean sinful humans, it lifts us to the company of our peers, the prophets and saints, the Joshuas and Judiths, the Esthers and Peters, the martyrs and poets. We are called to the same greatness as they, because we too are redeemed. The moral life can thus become not a matter of slavishly following rules, but of celebrating all we have been given and behaving like children of the king and queen. How can I act as less than I am?

Sweeping down the castle staircase, I longed for a proper tiara and train and wanted to whisper my thanks, "Morning, Dad." It may sound arrogant, but it is true: religion at its best houses human beings in a setting that befits their creator, and their own amazing scope. The gospel awakens us and calls us to be more than we ever dreamed we could become. If we believe that words addressed to Jesus also call to us, then Simeon's soaring invitation comes to our children: "And you, child, will be called the prophet of the Most High; for you will go before the Lord to prepare his ways..." (Luke 1:76).

The symbolic language of the church connects us to the abundance of the natural world, for at least an hour on Sunday. The best religious art uses the enduring elements of creation: brass and beeswax, copper and crystal, clay and wood. When we receive communion, it doesn't come in a Styrofoam cup. We drink from golden chalices or exquisite pottery, and the wine isn't watered down for the children.

In robust ritual, we draw our symbols from nature: waterfall and flower, bonfire and brass, bread and wine. Our words are not the flat exchanges of "Hi-how-are-you?" or the trite "have a good day," but blessings and invocations that sound more like courtly language. Symbol and gesture are lavish and large: anointing with fragrant oil that smells delicious for days afterward, cleansing with warm waters, extravagant hugs.

I like these goals for faith formation: "the education of longing" and "landscaping the religious imagination." Both descriptions are evocative and open-ended rather than narrow and dogmatic; both phrases might roam at home in a palace. To children who long for a larger world, who find their proper element exploring castles or creation, we cannot give less than what they deserve.

If our children hear legends of giants and heroes, they will yearn to be like them, to take their rightful places in this company. To educate their longing may mean helping them see that the shopping malls and video arcades, however pleasant, will never reward their deepest cravings. "You were made for more," we must say, then help them to claim their rich heritage of story and symbol, their identity as "children of promise" (Rom. 9:8).

When Dan suspected a dragon in the courtyard, it may have been due to the power of suggestion. Our biblical stories have the same evocative power, giving the youngest and oldest audiences the confidence that as Jesus acted, so you can act. His compassion and tenderness and power can also be yours. It's our job to present these gospel stories with the best flair and deepest insights we can.

Paul Philibert explains his theory of landscaping the religious imagination. "Just as the environment in which we live is designed and intended to give us a feeling of beauty and pleasure in our surroundings, so also is our psychic environment shaped by symbols.... The field of imagination is the yard or garden where our symbols flourish;...landscaping that terrain of images is obviously of enormous significance."[26] "The marvel of Christian liturgy is that "it binds up our inner needs with the symbols of God's presence and love."[27] Our hungers for meaning and touch, for beauty and order, for affirmation and challenge can be met in a church that tells stories, blesses, anoints, embraces and feeds, lights candles and places flowers on wheat-colored linen, sings and calls forth to service.

Sainthood may sound too pious as a goal for Lady Margaret or Lord Dan. But to live out of thankfulness, alert to the gifts of the most high king, to act with nobility — now there's a goal that shimmers like a dragon's scales, that wraps around the heart like mist around the turrets, that dances in the imagination like music on the dulcimer.

PART III

Guiding the Quest

We may know how to run a corporation, a catering service, or a classroom, but spirituality seems like murky water to many folks. Clarity may come in different forms: formal religion, ritual and prayer, retreats, stories of the saints, celebration of feasts, or Scripture. What helps one family may discourage another, because the quest for God is unique to every family configuration. The marvelous variety of families speaks of God's infinite creativity, tapering to each individual the special blessings we enjoy or challenges we meet. While one family's quest forms the basis for these chapters, our way has been infinitely enriched by the stories of other families. To those who have shared their experiences here, the deepest gratitude.

— 15 —

THE PESKY QUESTION
OF CHURCH

MOST of this book's focus has been on the informal, serendipitous things that can happen at home to bring parents and
children closer to the deity. Indeed, most profound belief is commu-
nicated at home; no institution can exert more than 10 percent of the
family's influence. But what about formal religion? Should a family
participate in church services regularly? Yes and no.

Surely Jesus learned most of his religious practice at home and
transformed what he saw there into the images of salt and lamps,
yeast and sparrows, that have shaped most Christians. From his
mother he learned a reflective stance; from his father may have come
his allusions to the green wood and the dry. Jewish religious practice
was firmly rooted in the home, where the family lit candles, read the
Torah, sang psalms, and consumed ritual meals.

On the other hand, the temple (the center for more formal religion) was often an unhappy place for Jesus. He drove the traders out
because he saw them corrupting God's house, turning it into a "den
of thieves." In turn, the scribes and Pharisees suspected him of being
a threat to traditional teaching and were influential in securing his
death sentence.

To what extent our own questions about institutionalized religion
parallel Jesus' troubles with the temple is of course an individual
matter. But it seems universally true that when parents and children
launch into God, the voyage may take them beyond conventional
pieties and established forms of religiosity. This terrible freedom can
threaten our security; in contrast, the church with its predictable
routines may seem to offer safe harbor.

Richard Rohr explains that humans tend to fear what we cannot
measure or contain. An approach to God which cannot be legislated
or listed, but instead occurs serendipitously in unexpected places
may seem so risky that we give it up and retire to the snug con-
fines of church. So, before Pentecost, the disciples once padlocked

the doors of the upper room. During traumatic or troubled times, that may be the appropriate response for us too. But eventually, the sunlight on the shore beckons again. As Rohr puts it, "Fortunately, God has grown used to our small and cowardly ways. God knows that we settle for easy certitudes instead of gospel freedom. And God is determined to break through."[28]

Should a parent then reject structures and launch this voyage independently? To some extent, yes. We do not want to be guilty of the criticism Rohr levels against mindless church-going. He charges that because we cannot tolerate what God offers, a love relationship that is "too near, too lavish too spacious," we surrender our freedom. We give up, deciding that "it's easier just to go to church."[29]

Any parent who takes on the quest for God with a child is assuming an independence that might have shocked a previous generation, with its staunch reliance on the professionals for expertise in matters of belief. Furthermore, most parents today hope that their children will develop a questioning faith, which thinks long and hard about issues rather than simply absorbing oracular pronouncements from on high. If we adopt a questioning stance, we may find ourselves at odds with religious institutions that value conformity over individual conscience. Yet many people (myself included) still turn regularly to the faith traditions that nourished their parents and grandparents. Why?

Like anything else, it's a question of balancing the positives against the negatives. My children, like most kids, have writhed in boredom at church, although none pushed it quite to the point of my friend's son, who in a fit of pique bellowed from the balcony onto the assembly below: "I don't like church!" escalating to: "And I don't like Jesus!" As each child approaches a "certain" age, we've restaged the battle over "Why do we hafta go to church?" My husband leans toward the clear-cut "that's our expectation while you live here," while I tend to shudder at the oxymoron "coerced faith." Much of my energy in the last few years has been directed toward church reform, with a particular concern for the enforced passivity children must endure every Sunday.

Yet having said all that, I still attend church regularly. Part of my motivation is the inability to answer Peter's question to Jesus, "But where else would we go?" No matter how cozy our home or how stunning our mountain scenery, it still doesn't hold a candle to the power of someone laying down his life for us and continuing to feed us with a bread and wine transformed into himself. Despite the frequency of dismal preaching, male-dominated rites, exclusive language, an apathetic assembly, and an unimaginative clergy, something keeps pulling me back.

Perhaps as a writer, I relate to novelist Gail Godwin's insistence that writing is a discipline, not an inspiring angel alighting on one's shoulder. Doggedly, she pursues her craft in season and out. Asked why, she replied: "What if the angel came and I weren't there?" Church can be the same: every now and then, the angel shows up. I don't want to miss the moment. Nor do I want my kids to miss those rare and wonderful experiences. Maybe some examples will show what I mean.

At one Easter Vigil, I finally understood what the experts mean by "liturgical catechesis," or the power of the symbols to speak. A dramatic storyteller had memorized the story of the Israelites crossing the Red Sea. Furthermore, he invited us to join in on the sung refrain, clapping loudly to "Horse and chariot were cast into the sea!" Perhaps it was the combination of darkened church, roaring bonfire, and storytelling by candlelight that drew my youngest daughter into the ancient tale.

Then, when the time came for baptism, Katie chose a front-row seat. As she watched a girl her own age being baptized, she squinted and flinched in sympathy. The waters pouring over the other child's head might have been drenching hers; she was one of the first to welcome the newest member of the community. The following January, having escaped winter and flown to Florida, Katie rolled down the car window and breathed in warm air. "Ah," she smiled. "It smells like Easter."

Perhaps such moments could have come without the church-going habit, but I'm not sure. Against the church's many failures I hold up one stunning success. The children of the Middle Ages walked through squalor and experienced rampant disease. Yet they could look up and see the spire of Salisbury cathedral, the windows of Notre Dame. In all the muck, the church held aloft some beauty.

So in the worst neighborhood of Los Angeles, the church offered a haven from the violence and brutality of the riots several years ago. It was not unusual for people to spend all Sunday afternoon in church, escaping hot, noisy, and overcrowded homes. There, they could count on the beauty of flower and candle, song and art to remind them that all creation is graced, and that material things can mediate God's goodness.

The aesthetic dimension of church is captured by novelist Mary Gordon, who criticizes much of her early formal religious experience but, in the Irish expression, "gives the divil his due." "The rhythmic, repetitive cadences of formal prayer"[30] instilled in her a love for strongly rhythmic prose which eventually defined her career. As a child, she was not conscious of the way she was absorbing from liturgy a sense of drama, rhetoric, and an "elaborate and varied and supple use of language."[31] Her images of prayerfulness, even in adulthood, are sensuous: the sounds and odors of religious life. Finally, she concludes, the exclusivity of her childhood church gave an aspiring novelist one of the greatest treasures she could have: "a secret world," rich in symbol, custom, and rite.[32]

All very well, one might harrumph, for children who will become novelists. What about garden variety kids? Gordon adds three more inherited blessings: the sense of comedy that always springs from the gap between the ideal and the real, images of heroic women, and a sense of high purpose. She knew early on that she was supposed to be a saint; nothing less would do. "Everything mattered terribly and you could never do enough."[33] Too heavy a burden to lay on a child? Quite the contrary. Gordon believes that parents cheat their children when they don't support their natural sense of seriousness and express high expectations for them.

Children whose days vacillate between video arcades and shopping malls are robbed of this challenge. Children who have every material need satisfied still have deeper yearnings. In James Carroll's story "The Sweet Taste of Childhood" the children get their wish — ice cream forever! Everyone is happy in the kingdom of ice cream. But something is missing: the anticipation of waiting for the ice cream truck's bells. The children have lost "a coming to long for and listen to. Something to yearn for, or better, a wandering man to love."[34]

To children living in some parts of Asia, Africa, and Latin America, our children must seem like those who live in the kingdom of ice cream. Yet in its universality, the church can stand as a beacon to children all over the world. To those in poverty or war zones, the church can represent safety, order, and beauty in a world gone berserk. A child in El Salvador during the civil war there once drew a picture of the local church and labeled it, "the place where the people come when the bombs fall."

A Jesuit missionary working in the refugee camps of Kenya writes of a prayer service there: "These people who are always sick, never well-fed, living in mud huts without water, prey to every whim of the police, far from their countries, facing uncertain futures, nevertheless thank God for the graces they have received. They are so joy-filled it is impossible not to be caught up in it — unmerited grace." In the refugee camps of Rwanda, the children come running with a cry of greeting, "Komera!" It means "have courage" and has been the common greeting in Rwanda for as long as anyone can remember.

Children living in the relative affluence of the U.S. or Canada can learn much from Deng, whose name means "holy." Because he yearns for education, he walks four hundred miles from the Sudan to Kenya. Parents can surely empathize with Rachel, the mother of a three-month-old baby. While the U.N. explicitly forbids the forced repatriation of refugees, in practice they are often harassed by the police. These brutal thugs care little about splitting families in their massive roundups and arrests. So Rachel, separated from her infant, sobs not only in pain with swollen breasts, but with fear for her missing child.

Ideally, the broader, global perspective that comes from belonging to a worldwide religion can turn to action. Fortunately, many projects are concrete and accessible to children. Parents can be grateful that whatever funds they contribute to these organizations are returned a hundredfold in benefits to their children, who learn from their participation to think beyond themselves and gratifying their immediate needs.

The Heifer project is an effort to purchase livestock for poor families; children get concrete reminders with small, cow-shaped erasers. For one hundred dollars, the Jesuit Refugee Services can keep a child in elementary school for a year.

Through the Christian Foundation for Children and the Aging, our youngest daughter has become a pen pal to Yina, whose family lives in a tin-roofed shack in Colombia on $80 a month. When Katie once wanted an $80 doll and we compared it to a family's monthly income, she quickly saw the dichotomy. Part of her allowance, earned from chores around the house, goes toward Yina, and when she receives a picture or letter in the mail, she folds the laundry or sweeps the kitchen with renewed zest.

Many North American children think of a bad hair day as a major crisis; their world revolves around the latest fad. Through Operation Rice Bowl, traditionally held during Lent, children can become engaged in more global activities. A family's contributions to a small cardboard rice bowl can help fund projects in forty-five countries. Children who place flag pins on these nations can get a lesson in geography as well as an appreciation for the scope of their influence.

Clean water is an amenity we tend to take for granted. In many countries, fetching water is the woman's responsibility, delegated to the children. Bringing a water pump into a village not only offsets the gastrointestinal diseases that kill many children each year; it also frees the children's time so they can attend school.

Our links to the rest of the world are not guilt trips we foist on our children, but lessons adults learn again and again. Recently, I was talking with a priest friend about the slow progress some women have made in liturgical participation. I lamented the fact that while we have made strides in other areas, we still seem to "sit at the back of the bus" when it comes to taking our places at the altar.

He smiled ruefully and told me two stories. One occurred in Africa, where he had encouraged a man to get medical attention for his wife, who was pregnant with the fourth child and critically ill. The doctor warned that if she did not rest, she risked losing both the baby and her own life. This created a dilemma for the husband and father. In his culture, it was unthinkable for a man to carry water. If his wife rested, how would the family get its water supply? Several days later, he greeted the priest joyfully. He had solved the problem! The American Jesuit jumped to other conclusions before the man told his: he had gotten his wife a smaller bucket.

Another incident occurred in a Middle Eastern country where a man allowed his wives to walk before him. The other men criticized him: did the women not know their rightful place behind their husband?

"No," he answered. "I have them walk before me as protection. In this area, there are rumors of land mines."

"Touché," I told my friend. "Nothing like a global nudge to restore my own issues to proper perspective." What the stories did for me can also happen for my children — and belonging to a catholic (that's deliberately a small "c") religion can help give them that international vision.

Perhaps the final word on formal religion, as on most topics, comes from the story: this one of the rabbi and the soapmaker who went on a walk together. The soapmaker complained that religion was no good. "After thousands of years teaching about goodness, after all the prayers and sermons, the world still suffers miserably. Why has religion had so little effect?"

The rabbi said nothing. They continued walking until they saw a child playing in the gutter.

"Look at that child!" he said then. "Soap should clean people, but the child is filthy. What good is soap?"

The soapmaker protested, "But soap can't do any good unless it is used."

"Exactly," said the rabbi. "So it is with Judaism or any other religion. It is ineffective unless it is applied and used."[35]

We do well to remember this story when we gauge our relationship to church. Churchgoers, like everyone else, are consumers. No longer will people put up with a church that fails to meet their needs simply because it's convenient — or mandated. So parents shop for a place where their families belong, where they and their children are nurtured. Many people put up with trade-offs: the music is lousy, but the youth group is dynamite; the sermons are like sedatives, but the community is hospitable and the children always get a special blessing. Some folks may be fortunate enough to have everything, but the search for the perfect church may be doomed to the same unreality as the search for the perfect school or the perfect surfing wave.

But as the rabbi reminds us, we cannot judge a church without also evaluating our participation in it. What have we done to make a faith community more alive, more sensitive to the needs of families with children, more attuned to the world's poor? Perhaps the questions bring us back to the beginning: we can't have overly high expectations for an institution whose role is that of first mate. On a personal voyage toward God, we and our children wear the captains' hats.

— *16* —

OARS FOR THE BOAT

THE SAME TWO WORDS that guided our exploration of church help balance the boat we launch into God. They function like oars, these words: yes and no. While the complexity of our lived experience cannot be reduced to monosyllables, the words serve as helpful handles, wedges to understanding this voyage that parents and children share. As with other chapters, this one serves as a prompt to start the reader's reflections. Every family will want to contribute their own "yeses" and "nos," personalizing this list of priorities.

For starters, "yes" to compassion and the importance of parenting, to creativity, celebration, and rest. Surely no virtue can bless the life of a family more than compassion. At home we can read each other with an accuracy found in no other setting. We know Amy is cranky from lack of sleep, or Jamal is lashing out at his younger sister because of his baseball team's losing streak. From caring parents, children can learn how to empathize. This quality cannot emerge without a painful period of being the center of the universe, and traces of this egocentricity linger throughout adolescence and adulthood. But those who are fortunate gradually learn compassion from those who excel at it. When I don't know the parents of our teenagers' friends, I can guess a lot: the kids willing to run errands, shoot basketballs with younger siblings, give each other rides, and sacrifice their own wants now and then must have strong role models at home.

Sometimes compassion doesn't look as soupy and sentimental as we might expect. Sometimes it can be tough as steel. For Nicholas's second Christmas, he asked for crutches. When he got to preschool, he could explain to other children, "My legs don't work well because I have spina bifida." By the time he was five, his seven-year-old sister had learned from her parents to emphasize the positive rather than cater to the negative. She decided to hide the crutches.

"I know you can do it," she'd say. "Walk to me, Nicholas!" When he would wobble thirty feet toward her, the older sister whooped a "Yes!" of encouragement.

Like anyone who believes in what they're doing, we voice a loud "yes" to the importance of parenting. We affirm over and over that it's a task deserving of energy and time. One dad, clearly committed to his children, hangs on his office wall two sayings. The first comes from Genesis 44:20: "His father loves him very much," and the second comes from an anonymous source:

> One hundred years from now it will not matter what my bank account was, the sort of house I lived in, or the kind of car I drove. But the world may be different because I was important in the life of a child.

We may never know how important we were. But Marian Wright Edelman, founder and president of the Children's Defense Fund, remembers how her parents and extended family protected her against racism: "We black children were wrapped up and rocked in a cradle of faith, song, prayer, ritual, and worship which immunized our spirits against some of the meanness and unfairness inflicted on our young psyches by racial discrimination and poverty in our segregated South and acquiescent nation."[36] The challenges we face now may be different, but we must still keep that cradle intact.

Life in the twentieth century is often stressful; both parents and children can labor beneath intolerable burdens. We worry about internal and external pressures and whether we are planting the seeds in our children that will carry them into the next millennium. Yet to wallow self-indulgently in anxiety becomes its own reward. People with martyr complexes, prune faces, and perfectly folded hands make me nervous. From my children I have learned how play can be prayer.

A child has the natural gifts of simplicity, presence, and wonder that adult contemplatives work hard to develop. Praise of the Lord does not always leap easily to adult lips. Children may not use religious jargon, but they can admire God's handiwork in the perfectly pitched baseball, a muddy tulip tip, a whirling hummingbird, or a sloppy kiss.

When I companion them best, I act like Miriam playing her tambourine, David dancing before the ark, or the glad spirit of creation: "I was his delight, playing before him always, rejoicing in his inhabited world and delighting in the human race" (Prov. 8:30).

Children seem to be constantly creating: art projects heavy with paste, constructions of blocks or Legos or Popsicle sticks. Unlike many adults, they are not paralyzed by the need to achieve perfection; their work is play. As Pablo Picasso says, "Every child is an artist. The problem is how to remain an artist once he grows up."[37] Perhaps there is hope for parents: if we hang around children long enough, their joyous creativity will be contagious. Then we may also learn from them two valuable lessons, summed up by Joseph Chilton Pearce: "To live a creative life, we must lose our fear of being wrong,"[38] and "we must accept that this creative pulse within us is God's creative pulse itself."[39]

"Yes" to family meals, no matter how much work they take, and birthday cakes, and all the quirky celebrations that spring as spontaneously as daisies throughout the year. Stability is important, but everyone likes variety in the secure routine. Forget elaborate planning — celebrations can be as simple as a mom who stuck a maraschino cherry on top of ice cream to praise Friday.

Busy, overstimulated parents can forget that children have fairly dull routines. Repeatedly they follow the same orbit of school, playground, and home. That's where the church year comes in handy: it's a treasury of seasons and cycles, feasts and fasts, highs and lows. With a calendar listing these events, there is almost always something to celebrate. As the mystic Hildegard of Bingen wrote in the fourteenth century, "Be not lax in celebrating. Be not lazy in the festive service of God. Be ablaze with enthusiasm."

The home is the original matrix for celebration; there the child first blows out the candles on the birthday cake. In church, the child may stare at the backs of heads and hear incomprehensible language. At home, the translation can occur. There we make connections between the ritual and the lived reality. If we fail to do so, we run the risk of passing on empty gestures.

Returning home from church one Sunday, Katie protested loudly about the boredom of the service. So Colleen and I improvised around the day's gospel: the wedding feast of Cana. We three created a wedding album for the Cana couple by drawing pictures and placing them in a photo album. That prompted Katie to ask about Mom and Dad's wedding album, so we explored that facet of her heritage. We concluded by cutting out water jars from construction paper, then listing our concerns on them. "Here's where we need Jesus to turn water into wine," I explained. We listed poverty, war, child abuse, AIDS, and other concerns, then lifted them up in prayer.

Our religious rituals don't make much sense if they are not grounded in celebrations at home. For instance, the Eucharist must seem foreign to children who eat meals in front of television sets. To appreciate it, they need the experience of sitting around a table where failure and fruitfulness sit close enough to pass the butter. One child may fret over a bad grade; another exults in a soccer goal. A parent recounts a business decision while a daughter peels a sunburn. In a context where people share their joys and sorrows, the paschal mystery of dying and rising can take on meaning.

Rest is a necessary corollary to celebration, the white space that frames the picture. Just as God rested on the last day of creation, families need room to breathe. Often we are overscheduled, with play practice, PTA meetings, band, sports, Scouts, and overtime at work. Yet the spiritual life cannot flourish without quiet time for doing nothing. Such idleness runs counter to a workaholic culture, but it contains a biblical wisdom: while the farmer seems to do nothing, the seed grows and sprouts (James 5:7–8).

How can we ever appreciate the biblical metaphor of the well-dressed lilies if we do not spend time admiring the birds of the air and flowers of the field? As Sue Bender points out, when we don't have fallow time, a deeper intelligence won't come forth. A pause, even a small pause, is a "little Sabbath to replenish the body and spirit."[40]

What happens if we don't take rest time? We may discover first-hand how heaven rewards, but hell motivates. People who have developed serious diseases related to exhaustion or overload learn this lesson the hard way. One victim writes, "Resting when exhausted was never on my list of possibilities. Resting when exhausted is now on my list of possibilities."[41]

Another says, "I don't know how to relax. I don't know how to just hang out. I don't have the vaguest notion of how to play. I have been the little adult my whole life. I came out of my mother's womb and began house cleaning....I never had anyone teach me how to hang out and have fun. Anytime I try to have a good time and play with friends, I am filled with anxiety and guilt."[42] In startling contrast, the saints admit freely to a propensity for napping. Thérèse of Lisieux confesses in her autobiography that she had slept through her prayers for seven years running. She adds, "Well, I am not desolate. I remember that little children are as pleasing to their parents when they are asleep as well as when they are wide awake." (Maybe more so!)

When one of the desert fathers was asked what to do about people dozing at prayer, he replied that he simply settled the sleeper's head in his own lap. Psalm 131 describes the creature resting in the Creator, intimate and secure as a child in a mother's lap:

> It is enough for me to keep my soul still and quiet,
> like a child in its mother's arms,
> as content as a child that has been weaned. (Ps. 131:2)

We can overhear the same sigh of deep content as God looked over creation and found it good. We can find the same satisfaction as we and our children rest in the God who made us, the God we long for.

While I'm not certain how to define the relationship, I suspect that "yes" and gratitude must be first cousins. Legends praise the gifts that fairies bring children at their christenings; surely one of the best gifts would be a grateful attitude.

Psychologist Charles Shelton, S.J., writes: "When we experience gratitude we come to know ourselves as valued and accepted. The kindness and sacrifice of another inform us of our own intrinsic worth."[43] To put this in terms relevant to children, they know that they are worthwhile people because someone else has been willing to sacrifice their time, their money, or their energy for them. On a spiritual plane, our gratitude to people can be enlarged into gratitude toward God, the source of all gifts. Relishing the fact that we are gifted by God can bring us to a sense of profound well-being, a positive basis for good mental health. In turn, it motivates us to want to reciprocate: the child who has been gifted searches for ways to return the favor.

Perhaps this dynamic is best illustrated by a story. Betsy Wack, now president of the school board in Clayton, Missouri, and the mother of five children, recalls how as an adolescent she would awaken on Saturday mornings sure that her dad would get her to the gym for basketball practice at 9:00. She'd climb eagerly into the car, only to find two or three or four siblings, all needing to be somewhere at 9:00, with the locations often different and far apart.

She'd arrive at the gym, though not at 9:00, and wouldn't miss the few moments of practice she had lost. She'd awaken the following Saturday certain that her dad would get her to the gym at 9:00. Betsy writes in retrospect, "I live out my childhood with a dad who always says 'yes,' always thinks he can, always tries, and often does."

"Then I become a parent who rushes to the car and finds three or four children, all wanting to be different places at the same time, and I say 'yes,' and I think I can and try, and often do. Will my children remember the times I failed and become adults who need to control their 'yesses'? Or will they awake to find two or three children all needing a 'yes,' all deserving a 'yes,' all accepting when it doesn't work? Did Dad understand that he was teaching me to say 'yes,' and that basketball was incidental? Or did he have a mother or a father who always said 'yes,' and always tried and often succeeded?"

Psychologists point to the human quirk of remembering hurts longer than blessings, of concentrating more on one negative comment than on hundreds of positive ones. Yet they have also studied the ability to counter this natural tendency. We need not be paralyzed by negative emotions if we can recall positive experiences to offset them.

Again, the psychological insights may be easier to understand in terms of examples. A mother explained how her family endured crises: "We admit that things may look terrible at the moment, but we're glad we still have each other. We don't focus on the stress; we concentrate on the relationships built over the long haul."

She went on to describe a traumatic scene in a doctor's office, where she and her eight-year-old son awaited his diagnosis. He lay swathed in white on the examining table; she stood close by, her heart in her throat as the doctor examined the x-rays. Precisely at the moment of the worst tension, her son looked up at his mom and stuck out his tongue. She, of course, reciprocated; the dark cloud shadowing them dissolved in laughter.

It may not be such a far stretch to the Bible, a record of throbbing emotion and fleshly humanity. The story of Job is especially appealing because the hero is a husband and father. In the modern version *J. B.*, a play by Archibald MacLeish, the audience meets the hero at Thanksgiving dinner, where he happily carves turkey, drinks wine, and banters with his wife and children. She prods him to be more conscious of counting blessings; he counters, "Nobody *deserves* it, Sarah: Not the world that God has given us,"[44] and continues,

> "The thanks are
> part of love and paid like love:
> Free gift or not worth having."[45]

When Job loses his property and children, his home and health, he is devastated. As he sits in the ashes, covered with sores, his wife wants him to curse God. Yet Job replies, "Shall we receive the good at the hand of God, and not receive the bad?" (Job 2:10). He mourns the times when he enjoyed the friendship of God, "when my children were around me" (29:5). Depressed by the "windy words" of his "comforters" (the term is used ironically), he has the audacity to declare, "I would speak to the Almighty, and I desire to argue my case with God" (13:3).

God enters into the discussion, revealing to Job "things too wonderful for me, which I did not know" (42:3). In the playwright's words,

> The whole creation! And God showed him!
> God stood stooping there to show him!
> God with all those stars and stallions!
> He with little children's bones![46]

In spite of his losses, Job marvels at God's power and comes to peace, even before his fortunes are restored. While he does not deny the tragedy, he realizes that both what was given and what was taken were touched by the hands of the same loving God.

"No" enters the vocabulary with the ferocity of a two-year-old; at around that age parents may realize with a sinking feeling that love cannot be uncritical. This child we loved so purely and wholeheartedly now seems hell-bent on self-destruction; only our "no" stands between him and the electrical outlets. If previously our love was sentimental, "no" gives it backbone and definition.

The mother of a physically challenged child, on a long car trip with her daughter and her own friend, once repeatedly denied the child's requests for a bathroom stop. The other adult was astonished: How could the mother be so heartless? The mother explained firmly that she knew her daughter's limits; to cave in too soon would do the little girl no favors.

The father of a child in a wheelchair rules out negative language. "We don't talk about what he can't do, but what he can do. We don't use the vocabulary of 'never,' but talk in terms of 'anything is possible.' Simply because the child uses a wheelchair doesn't mean he can't bat and throw. When all his cousins play softball, they make sure that someone pushes the wheelchair to the base, and allow a little extra time for him to get there."

Moving beyond the family circle, we find a whole range of injustices to which we must say "no," protecting not only our own children but all children. "No" to a culture so geared to productivity that it hangs a dollar value on everything, that cannot understand the human need to watch clouds form pictures or spiders spin webs. Inasmuch as they are able, parents must send a clear "no" to corporate policies which run roughshod over families, requiring overtime and constant moves, all in the name of efficiency. It's a pernicious Catch-22 which makes these demands at the same time it undermines peoples' motivation to work: precious time with their families. In an anxious economy, people tend to make enormous sacrifices to keep their jobs, keenly aware that providing their children with financial security may at the same time be draining them of the emotional security they need as much if not more.

On a national scale, parents are the natural ones to say "no" to government proposals that jeopardize the health and education of our children so that we can pour more funds into expensive weapons. A classic case demonstrates how a prophetic, nonviolent stance can have its roots in the squabbles of family life. Trappist monk and author Thomas Merton recognized the possibility of a nuclear holocaust long before most people suspected the threat of such a cataclysm. He called militarism "the greatest and most agonizing issue of our time." While his prophetic "no" has been widely acclaimed, few people know the story that may underlie it.

Merton's younger brother, John Paul, was sweet and serene; "everyone was impressed by his constant and unruffled happiness."[47] Orphaned at an early age, the two boys lived for a while with their grandparents in Douglaston, New Jersey.

Typical of the older brother, Tom preferred the company of his buddies to his younger brother's. When his gang built huts in the woods, John Paul was an embarrassing burden. Merton recalls poignantly how they tried to drive him away by throwing stones:

> The picture I get of my brother John Paul is this: standing in a field...is this little perplexed five-year-old kid in short pants..., standing quite still, with his arms hanging down at his sides, and gazing in our direction, afraid to come any nearer on account of the stones, as insulted as he is saddened, and his eyes full of indignation and sorrow. And yet he does not go away. We shout at him to get out of there, to beat it, and go home, and wing a couple of more rocks in that direction, and he does not go away. We tell him to play in some other place. He does not move.
>
> And there he stands, not sobbing, not crying, but angry and unhappy and offended and tremendously sad....The law written in his nature says that he must be with his elder brother, and do what he is doing: and he cannot understand why this law of love is being so wildly and unjustly violated in his case.[48]

The profound effect of that episode is clear from all the detail Merton remembers many years later; indeed, the scene would haunt him the rest of his life. With a terrible irony, his brother was killed in World War II and buried at sea. From this personal tragedy may have sprung Merton's "nos" to war. Did he see modern weaponry as a disastrous magnification of the stones thrown at Douglaston? Did his empathy for war's victims begin with a five-year-old boy, and a slightly older pilot buried in the North Sea? Did he know the brotherhood of all humanity from his ties with John Paul?

The sibling rivalries and interactions that fill our homes may seem petty, until we see their long-range effects in a case as dramatic as this one. Hence, we can't say an authentic "no" to global warfare until we have first made our homes into violence-free zones. Eliminating physical violence may sound obvious, until we start thinking about other ways we do violence: with thoughtless words that "put down" our children, with smug assumptions that we know best because we're bigger, with impatience about hearing their sides of the story.

William Faulkner once wrote good advice for families: "Some things you must never stop refusing to bear. Injustice and outrage and dishonor and shame. Not for kudos and not for cash. Just refuse to bear them." Such a "no" can become a loud "yes" to God and each other.

— 17 —

GOD OF THE SILENT SPACE

WHILE MANY FAMILIES know the need for quiet times and sacred spaces, it's hard to honor that need in practice. We find it difficult to justify time away from home, or a priority given to prayer. Unless we are fortunate enough to live near a place like Sacred Heart Retreat House, Sedalia, Colorado....

Inventory the sleepy town, and you'll find one stoplight at the only intersection, one barely hyphenated Gas – Diner – Auto Parts – Grocery Store, one bar, one restaurant, and a human population outnumbered by four-footed critters.

Just west of this little clump called town stands the retreat center. There, cattle lounge in the long grass and lush gardens enfold the peach tones of sunset. On five hundred acres in the foothills of the Rockies, paths meander and hummingbirds guzzle the abundant iris. The large living room has a huge fireplace and comfortable reading chairs. But nothing in the unpretentious setting explains why on a global gauge, the place might register pulsing heat.

The activities in which people engage here seem unremarkable. The absence of business-as-usual might appear to violate some state or federal law, but retreatants pursue the difficult inner work of integration. They read, pray, walk, think, eat, sing, and rarely speak. The silence is so pervasive that a new kitchen worker thought the house hosted gatherings of only the speech-impaired. Yet that stillness is gestational. People leave here filled with pluck, humor, and peace. They are reenergized for ministries which affect countless others. With the unlikely wedges of prayer and song, they pry open forgotten truths. Those suffering from parent burn-out or ministry fatigue are revitalized by a mysterious grace. The poet May Sarton came closest to describing the dynamic when she wrote:

> ...where people have lived in inwardness
> The air is charged with blessing and does bless;
> Windows look out on mountains and the walls are kind.[49]

Retreatants rediscover the creature in whom God delights. Coming home to oneself in this way diminishes the power a crisis can have over us. Whether a project succeeds or fails becomes unimportant as we become convinced we have value over and above what we do for a living. We are just as precious to God when we sit in a meadow admiring a wildflower as when we conduct a workshop for a hundred people or make a business decision affecting thousands.

Franciscan Richard Rohr, explaining his motivation for entering a Lenten hermitage at Big Sur, said, "I had to find once again what it is that supports me. Who is it that names and loves me, and who is this naked man behind all his public words?"[50] Could this drive to reestablish identity as God's child be just as important for a parent? I once wondered. Could the kids survive for a few days without me — and could I get over the guilt of leaving them?

The answer to all three questions has turned out to be a resounding yes. This God of ours likes to hang out in places of beauty and quiet. It becomes almost antiphonal in the gospel: the alternation of Jesus going off to pray, with the crowds searching him out. Jesus must have been impelled by the knowledge that if all comes from God, we had best spend time with God replenishing the sources of grace.

Seeking God in a retreat setting, I have never been disappointed. In God's gracious way, my time and efforts are rewarded far more than I ever anticipate. Gradually, my children are learning that it's worth giving up Mom for a few days because she comes back a gentler, more centered person. My workaholic guilt is assuaged by writing more than I could at home, because my work there is uninterrupted.

I have wanted my books, articles, and talks to do more than reflect a fluency with words. I hope they will spring from the solid inner peace that wells in solitude. Surely one of the finest gifts any retreat house offers is that of leaving people alone. Thus, the conscientious, especially parents, can cherish a reprieve from duty. Gladly, they sink into a no-make-up, no-dress-up relaxation. In an empty stretch of time, no one yells, "Mom!" or hints at imminent starvation. Spaces which are still and empty can fill peacefully and surely with Presence.

When I come on retreat, a cacophony of inner voices stills. I tune out the hurtful ones: "Why didn't you pay that bill on time?" "How arrogant of you to write about women at the Last Supper!" "You're a lousy mom who doesn't give her kids enough time," replacing them with the only voice that matters saying, "You are my beloved daughter." If I do not claim that last one, do not believe it in my sinews, then I cannot walk freely through this world, cannot give anything to my children or anyone else.

To recover inner attention and reverence, I don't do anything particularly churchy here. I go for walks. I eat slowly, listening to music. I sleep and read luxuriously late at night or early in the morning without disturbing anyone. I smell lilacs spangled with dew and watch a display of stars that rivals any July 4th fireworks. I sink into long silences as rare to a mom as surplus cash after the orthodontist's bills. Gradually I start to feel fully alive, in the best sense of knowing I am the beloved of God, whose arms enclose me, whose spirit buoys me, whose love encircles me always. I drink deeply of a peace which words only trivialize, a bone-deep conviction of God's activity in my life.

I put most projects on hold, realizing they are good things I want to do, just not yet. Here the agenda is blessedly free: three to five days of nothing. Some people say it takes courage to plunge into the silence and solitude; for me it's like a fine wine that I sip slowly, eagerly. The only comparison I can make limps, but after the birth of our youngest child, I was hemorrhaging. Some kind nurse shot a dose of painkiller directly into my IV — instant bliss! Here, without drugs, the endless activity of the mind slows down; I am content to simply be.

Over time, I've come to see that this solitude is not a crutch or an escape. Rather, it is so vital that I must schedule it as regularly as exercise class or a medical check-up. A retreat is a high priority because it guarantees that what I give my family, friends, and colleagues is genuine, not phony. Having achieved some inner wholeness at the retreat house, I can cope with almost any crisis at home. The pattern has been repeated so often I've come to trust it: a steady movement from frenzy to peace, from feverish desperation to restored hope, from teeming need to tranquil gratitude.

Not that this is easy. It requires a deliberate disentanglement from all the paraphernalia of home, an advance attention to detail, and a husband willing to give me this gift and bear the load himself for a few days. But somehow, it keeps me sane, knowing the retreat house is there, forty miles away. After a few days of it, I carry it wherever I go, bringing its peace to office or convention center, kitchen or car pool.

In the ordinary routine, we have so many multiple experiences that it's easy to miss their meaning. Here, time slows down so we can appreciate the little things: the tawny color of wheat stalks beneath the winter sunlight, the intricate shapes of dried flowers, the coverlet of bird song at twilight, the comfort of hot tea and cookies after stargazing. The lines bend between beauty and prayer. I'm not always sure when I'm praying or not; maybe just appreciating God's presence is the best prayer.

"I have only one life," my retreat director reminds me subtly. She is a wise religious who prefers "savoring" to "racing through." Gradually, she leads me to a place where I can stand firm in my own truth, where I gain the courage to say "no." "You're not just dishing out hash to every comer," she counsels when the children's demands intensify. "When you are at peace within yourself, they recognize it. They can modify their greed for attention. And you don't have to do it all alone."

Despite Sister's persuasive logic, my youngest daughter has been hard to convince. Stubborn as her mother, she resists my absences even though she also enjoys the retreat center's hammock, rabbits, rainbows, fish, and cookie jar. Last time I phoned her from the retreat house, she harrumphed, "So — are you living an examined life?" I'd forgotten that in my last attempt to explain my compulsion for quiet time, I'd told her, "The unexamined life is not worth living."

I wish she'd had a parent-tot retreat when she was three or four. During a morning or afternoon with small children, a team of women from the retreat house teach children how to enter their "heart room," to find that inner place of peace no matter how rowdy things get at the day care center, no matter how crazy the ruckus at home.

Two sisters and two moms lead children to prayer through right-brain activity such as storytelling, art, and an imaginary field trip. With a little prompting, the children then close their eyes and picture Jesus. They lie on the floor and talk with him for a few moments. Their lips move silently; clearly some important communication goes on.

Down the hall, their parents make the same trip into their heart rooms. Their relief is palpable as they hear the reassurance, "Your child is having a special time with Jesus. Now it's time for your spiritual experience too. If Jesus himself had to withdraw from the constant demands at times, isn't it logical that you should also?" For a brief lull in a hectic week, parents pause to consider all that has colored their experience and made them unique. They call on the strength of the Spirit and the companionship of Jesus, who makes his home in us. They and their children learn to repeat this step-back-in-order-to-step-forward at home. After their retreat, one four-year-old gave her frazzled mother an *hour* of peace and quiet, comforting her with the assurance, "It's okay. You can go to your heart room any time!"[51]

How blessed are we, parents and children, who learn the value of the silent space and can join with God there. Early in life, children can come to prayer fresh; unlike jaded adults, they don't necessarily connect the word "retreat" with a fear-filled, dry, or compulsory experience. They can approach prayer with the enthusiasm Marian Cowan and John Futrell describe in *The Spiritual Exercises of St. Ignatius of Loyola:* "I am going to meet God; I am going to have a personal encounter with my one great Love."[52]

Nor is it too late for us, the parents who endured fire-and-brimstone high school retreats where French kissing ranked worse than serial killing. The retreat climate has improved dramatically and retreat directors are no longer dour or pompous. With their help, we can recover the jewel of the retreat experience and come to know intimately Richard Rohr's definition of prayer: "Prayer is sitting in the silence until it silences us, choosing gratitude until we are grateful, praising God until we ourselves are an act of praise."[53]

— *18* —

"Good Enough" Ritual
and Prayer

I ALWAYS THOUGHT that the Coffey family's report card on ritual and prayer would be pretty dismal. We believed in its importance: it is our duty to thank and praise; it gives children security and identity, and even helps heal children in alcoholic families. But when it came to practice, we seemed to have as little skill as we had for bumbling through Algebra.

I resented the long, formal prayers written by clerics who must not know the short attention span of hungry children squirming before a meal. Most of the books composed in convents overlook the fact that at one end of the dinner table, a sixteen-year-old is keeling over with boredom, while at the other, a two-year-old is sticking French fries up her nose. I sympathized with a friend who was intimidated simply by the materials list for staging family ritual events. When we gathered stiffly around the kitchen table for Advent wreath lighting or Lenten reflection, the language seemed forced and the kids looked wooden.

Then I learned that ritual could be larger than the narrow box I'd confined it to. The idea that parenting doesn't have to be perfect, but "good enough" brings tremendous relief to many parents who are painfully aware of their flaws. The same idea can be extended to include "good enough ritual."

One step in my liberation was discovering that Elizabeth Ann Seton, the first canonized American saint, had a terrible time praying for more than five minutes. Widowed at twenty-nine, she struggled to raise her five children under seven and her husband's orphaned brothers and sisters. She sounds like a modern mom juggling the phone, the baby, and a leaky dishwasher when she writes, "If I retire one moment, I hear a half dozen voices calling sister or mama." It comforted me immensely to know that she not only endured the trials of parenthood, she rode into heaven on them.

More words of relief came from Thomas Merton, the Trappist monk whom I'd always revered, if for no other reason than that he

105

stashed a six-pack in the wood pile behind his hermitage. In a conversation on prayer, he once slammed the table with his fist and said,
"If prayer is getting in your way, cut it out! Stop praying! Just BE
prayer!"[54]

When I see the stresses many families cope with and remain civ-
ilized, I think they are being prayer. I think they are being prayer
when my twenty-two-year-old son stays up all night packing his
twenty-year-old sister for college, and she reciprocates for his next
trip. I think she is being prayer when a seven-year-old places a single tulip in a cut-glass vase and breathes, "Alleluia." I think they are
being prayer when a family facing foreclosure on their home tries to
name the blessing in the pain and decides that they may not have
a wonderful house, but they'll still have a wonderful family. I think
they are being prayer when my friend Margie calls from work to ask
her ten-year-old what he'd like for his birthday. Hearing the fatigue
in her voice, he responds, "You're all the gift I need. Come home."

Perhaps an analogy to prayer springs from the dangerous passage
most parents make through their children's rooms to tuck them in at
night. We enter the room at risk, not knowing what slimy creatures
or pointy jacks menace our bare feet. Unable to see in the darkness,
we bumble toward the bed, convinced that we must cover the child
or kiss her goodnight.

The dangers don't deter us from our ultimate goal, because we
know that someone beloved breathes in the darkness. When we feel
a tiny toe or brush against wispy hair, we know that walking the obstacle course was worthwhile. If we are lucky, the child stirs, reaches
out a hand, or mumbles, "I love you, mom."

In the same way, our attempts at prayer may seem like feeble stabs
in the dark. We hesitate to begin because we know how soon we'll
be interrupted. Yet God waits at the end of the obstacle course, to
fill our silence with blessing. Surely the God who loves our children
infinitely more than we do shares the joy in them or concern for
them that prompts our prayer.

At special times, we pray more intentionally. It took some or-
chestration, but our whole family recently chimed in on prayer for
our oldest son, David, who was about to graduate from college and
join the ranks of the unemployed. Then he applied for a job which
seemed perfect. It would fit his skills and open doors for his career.
The only problem was the other 599 applicants, some of them flying
in from Harvard and Yale for interviews.

Clearly, the situation called for intensive prayer. I coordinated
time zones: the day of the first interview, my husband and youngest

daughter were home on mountain time, my older daughter was at college on Pacific time, and I was giving a talk on the east coast. Nonetheless, we all sent up simultaneous, heart-felt intercessions at the moment David walked into the interviewer's office.

Even more extraordinary was the contribution of our younger son. Ordinarily, Sean does not go out of his way to do teacher-pleasing things. But the day of the interview, a school holiday, he volunteered to sing with the choir for a funeral. He offered up a long, hot morning in an airless church. When David called to report that he thought the interview had gone badly, Sean commented, "Rats — all that torture wasted. I should have offered it up to get a car."

Despite David's initial misgivings, he was called for a second interview, and again the family joined in prayer. I hope it does not sound like superstition; surely his hard work and interviewing skills played their part in the successful second interview. Nor do we get stuck on only the prayer of petition. When David finally got the job, a mighty roar of gratitude went up from our home. Easter alleluias were too weak to capture our joy: it took a combination of dancing, shouting, and high fives to express it fully.

Perhaps we become prayer more often than we realize, so that St. Paul's exhortation to "pray always" is not as impossible and impractical as it sounds. Perhaps some of the practices that seem so ordinary we take them for granted are in fact ritual. As a liturgist (of all people!) once reminded me, "Most good ritual doesn't happen in church." To prove the point, he recounted the story of a man who had spent time in jail for resisting the draft. When his term was ended, his wife drove him directly from the prison environment to a lovely forest. She pulled off his clothes, cleansed him in the waters of a stream, rubbed his skin with sage. Her ritual was meant to wash away the terrible, demeaning treatment he had received in a sterile penal institution.

Or what could be more holy than the ritual devised by a ten- and thirteen-year-old to honor their parents' fifteenth anniversary? When Mom and Dad got home that day, tired from work, they found two banners draped across the living room. In their children's printing, one proclaimed, "I Sherwood take you Marianne to be my wife." The other read, "I Marianne take you Sherwood to be my husband." The two banners met in a corner over a table, where the children had arranged on a lace tablecloth their parents' wedding candle, photo album, some flowers — and a surprise gift certificate for a night at a local inn. The day after, Sherwood smiled, "How much more spiritual can we get? How much we all mean to one another...."

Our family rituals may not be so dramatic, but I hope they are planting some seeds and creating some memories in our children. I once made a retreat with a group of older women who spoke with nostalgia of the devotions that had meant much to them in childhood: novenas, statues, rosaries. None of these held any meaning for me. But I wondered whether, in jettisoning these pillars of the past, we had found anything to replace them. Will our children remember Sunday as free samples at the grocery store or Easter as new clothes? The horror of that vacuum has driven me to see some of our rituals in a better light and to introduce others into the family.

In a climate where seasons are clearly delineated, we often ritualize our farewell to the dying season and our welcome to the next. One year, the newspapers kindly warned us that the first blizzard of the year would arrive on Monday, but that the October weekend would remain balmy. We seized the opportunity to taste for a final time the best that summer had to offer. We would gather a brimming cornucopia of sense impressions like a glorious harvest that would carry us warmly into winter.

Our first stop was the botanic gardens, where chrysanthemums bloomed in shades of burgundy, vanilla, damson, and maize. We sniffed our way through the rose gardens like gluttons, deeply breathing the last of the year's fragrance. In the herb garden, we rubbed leaves of lavender, mint, and lemon verbena between our fingers, savoring their aromas. The children made earrings of snapdragons and tied bracelets of miniature red chiles.

They especially liked launching seed parachutes. Milkweed seeds lodge neatly in canoe-shaped husks. They propelled them forward with a solemn countdown: "5–4–3–2–1: Lift off!" Then they launched them over lakes and along air currents, so that as one season ended, another spring was set in motion. For the same reason, we plant bulbs every fall. Those purplish lumps may look unpromising but somehow turn into crocuses, hyacinths, and daffodils. Perhaps that transformation is every child's introduction to the possibilities of resurrection.

The first snow signals another ritual: soup for dinner, hot chocolate by the fire, flannel sheets on the beds. As winter melts away, our favorite ritual of spring is ripping off the ugly plastic that has clouded our windows and kept our heating bills down all winter.

We never fully appreciated our St. Nicholas Day ritual until a friend happened to spend the night before the feast with us. Sheila came from a wealthy but unhappy home and dreaded the coming Christmas holidays. She had never put her shoes out for the mythic saint to fill, but at sixteen she got her chance. Sheila aligned her tennies with the rest of the family's and waited eagerly.

No one could have guessed how a sixty-nine-cent pen, a two-dollar hair clip, and ninety-eight cents worth of candy could have filled a millionaire's daughter with such delight. When Sheila was baptized several years later, I wondered if a shoe filled for St. Nick's Day had played any part in her conversion.

Some of our regular rituals look less seasonal and more official. More clearly, they contain liturgist Bob Piercy's key ingredients of ritual: community, repetition, symbol, awe and wonder, and affirmation. Whenever a special event occurs in our family, we commemorate it with the blessing cup. One child fetches the earthenware goblet from the china closet, another fills it with juice or milk, and as we pass it around, all drinking from the same vessel, we pray, "Thank God for Katie's home run." "Thank you, God, for the birth of our new baby cousin." "Please help grandpa recover from surgery." "We all thank you for the new VCR!"

As trips begin or vacations end, our family joins hands and says together the Our Father, placing each other in God's care for the months before we gather again. Then we're off to college, work, travel, myriad activities — all the centrifugal energy having been gathered and blessed in one still center, the circle of our hands. The blessing that evolves over time is that with this, as with most good rituals, the kids pick up the beat when the parents forget or are too exhausted or frazzled to remember. What a relief when a new driver, behind the wheel for the first time, with all the family trembling and joking behind him, reaches out his hand to start the prayer.

One tradition the kids will probably never let us forget is the celebration of their feast days. Parents may groan at the thought of an unnecessary burden placed on an already full calendar. But it is every child's birthright to be part of a larger picture and belong to the community of saints. With a little research, it has not been hard to find the feast date of the saint for whom a child is named.

If Cookie or Brooke isn't on the canonized calendar, it's easy enough to use the middle name, or choose a saint with a special affinity. Rare is the child who'd quibble with the argument, "You'll just have to be the *first* St. Mandy!" Feast days aren't another excuse for consumerism; gifts are deliberately small or low key. But it's the perfect chance for a movie, video, tennis game, concert, or picnic. It may mean that younger children get to wear a construction-paper crown that says, "Feast Day Kid" or older ones get a trip to Dairy Queen. Kids who celebrate feast days *in addition to* birthdays quickly become the envy of others whose parents are not so enlightened. When an uncle visited our family on his feast day, the children made him a crown and a special dessert. Surprised by the attention, he said with moist eyes, "I wish I'd had this forty years ago.... "

While most folks know the importance of building healthy self-esteem, we may often get to the end of the day wondering if we said anything positive. We may want to hug a child and say, "I'm so lucky to have you." Instead we yell, "You're late for school!" or "Don't forget your lunch!" The feast day is an annual reminder that a person is precious and should be told. The Bible stresses that God calls us by name, a sign that we are special and unique. By celebrating feast days, we imitate the divine care.

A similar gesture, which can be repeated daily, is the blessing. Saying aloud our hope that our children have all the good things God intends for them has a long history. In Genesis, God promised Abraham and Sarah, "I will make of you a great nation, and I will bless you, and make your name great, so that you will be a blessing ... and in you all the families of the earth shall be blessed" (12:2–3)

Henri Nouwen writes in *The Life of the Beloved:*

> Children need to be blessed by their parents and parents by their children.... To give someone a blessing is the most significant affirmation we can offer. And more than that: to give a blessing creates the reality of which it speaks.... A blessing touches the original goodness of the other and calls forth his or her Belovedness.[55]

Simply marking the cross on children's foreheads or hands reminds them they are special and loved. We can use our own words or a formula like the sign of the cross or "May the blessing of God be upon you." In some cultures, a child cannot leave home for play or school without a blessing, and in New Mexico I learned the comfort of singing Carey Landry's "A Prayer of Blessing," recorded on the *Bloom Where You're Planted* audiocassette.

Often this practice comes back and surprises us: one morning, my husband graciously offered to entertain the children for the day so I could write uninterrupted. As they tumbled out the door and I headed for the computer, he said softly, "May what you do today be a blessing and blessed." One night when I crawled into bed, sick and exhausted, my youngest child blessed me.

The gift of blessing from Spanish-speaking people suggests that we may appreciate ritual more when we see it in other cultures, the Anglo matrix perhaps somewhat ritually impaired. That strikes me when I watch African-American dancers annually at the Los Angeles Religious Education Congress. They seem uninhibited as they dance in costumes of primary colors, their scarves swirling, their motions limber. Children are always part of the troupe, and I'll never forget one self-possessed little girl, her hair in a hundred braids, her garments a bright batik, who danced in the incense regally.

During a Bar or Bat Mitzvah, a whole cluster of grandparents, aunts, uncles, siblings, and friends surround the young boy or girl with their support. Publicly, the parents proclaim their pride in words that the youngster must carry throughout the rest of a lifetime. One mother spoke to her son in words every child should hear. (As Urie Brofenbrenner says, "Every child needs an adult who is absolutely crazy about him or her.")

If I'd known how resourceful you were, I wouldn't have worried so much when you got lost in the mall at twenty months.

If I'd known how thoughtful you were, I wouldn't have been so moved by your care for your dying grandfather at age seven.

If I'd known how bright you were, I wouldn't have been so surprised by your analysis of the State of the Union address at age nine.

If I'd known how poised you were, I wouldn't have been so stunned by your first public speaking engagement at eleven.

And if I'd known how much I would love you. . . .

The rest of the sentence got lost in tears, but there was no need to say it aloud. All the parents in the room were silently adding their own endings.

A bedtime ritual we've adapted comes from *Sleeping with Bread*. The authors explain that during the World War II bombing raids, many children were left orphaned and starving. The fortunate ones were rescued, sheltered, and fed. But despite their safe refuges, many of these children could not sleep at night. Nothing reassured them, until someone thought of giving each child a piece of bread to hold at bedtime. It worked: they fell asleep knowing, "I ate today; I will eat tomorrow."

The parallel the Linns propose is a form of the Ignatian examen. Before falling asleep, people ask themselves, "For what am I most grateful? For what am I least grateful?" The question can take other forms, such as "Where did I feel most alive today? least alive?" Where was I happiest/saddest?" Generally, God wants us to do more of the former; less of the latter. That's easy enough for children to understand. Over time, answers to the question follow a pattern: we learn what to seek and what to avoid. Gratitude for the day's gifts (*and* sadnesses) leads to the healing of the unconscious.[56]

One family who taught their children to do the examen regularly saw its benefits over time. Their children learned to trust themselves, to take ownership of their lives, and to share deep feelings. When I've used this ritual to close the day, my youngest daughter sometimes confides, "I had two 'bests' today!" Or she'll describe her discomfort when the other girls at school made fun of one girl's new haircut.

From the adult perspective, I'll sometimes find that a day which didn't seem spectacular did, in retrospect, contain enough crumbs to make a loaf. My list sometimes includes a phone call from a friend, a few moments watching the evening light fall on my geraniums, a stimulating read, fresh cherries for dessert, or a good joke.

This practice has other names: one family calls it P. J. Time, the last quiet chat of the day between parent and child. One mom was delighted to find that it gave a sensitive, introverted child a regular outlet to express the tensions he'd carry home from school every day, but didn't know how to release. Another child recited her "Bests and Worsts" in a cadence of "and then...," "and then..." that ended naturally with "Amen!"

Families who make "Best/Worst" times or blessing cups or feast days a regular part of their lives have been pleased to discover how their children want to share their particular practices with visitors. It is almost as if the children are saying, "This is where we belong. This is what we value. If you come to our home, this is our style."

Surely one component of "good enough ritual" is the ordinary routines we take so for granted that we would never classify them with that formal-sounding name. Waking, we can pray the psalm, "In the morning, you hear my voice; at dawn I will make ready and watch for you" (Ps. 5:3). Or we may echo the gratitude of Maya Angelou's grandmother on awakening: "Thank you that you didn't allow the bed I lay on last night to be my cooling board, nor my blanket my winding sheet."[57] People who do not live in circumstances as cushy as ours see a new day with wonder: for a family in Mexico, the first miracle is that the family and the world are still alive. The next miracle is the appearance of the sun, "la cobija de los pobres," the blanket of the poor.[58]

The morning shower is another opportunity for praise: washing off the dust of the previous day, we seize the opportunity to start over again, cleansed, fresh, confident. Or perhaps we dissolve the day's tensions in an evening bath, warm and fragrant, followed by the ritual dear to all children, a bedtime story and tucking in for the night.

One mother passed on to her children a special prayer from her childhood: "Thank you, God for seeing me safely through this day. Please continue to watch over me, guide me, and protect me in your loving way." Her little daughter became so attached to the prayer that she'd become upset when she spent the night with relatives who were unfamiliar with it. The day couldn't close properly without, "In Your Loving Way"!

As an adult, Lori Lippert recalled how her six siblings would be doing homework or preparing for bed in the evening. The youngest child, Lori would snuggle, warm and clean, between her parents in their large bed. Dad would read *Winnie-the-Pooh* aloud as Mom and Lori listened and giggled. As Eeyore reminded them that birthdays are, indeed, important days, Emily would appear at the door and crawl into the bed. The story continued, "about as big as Piglet ...my favorite size." Pretty soon, older brothers Chris and Chick appear. "Red...my favorite color," said Eeyore. Then Betsy capitulates, no longer able to resist the magic of Pooh for the equations of Algebra. By the time a "useful pot to put things in" has become a fine birthday present, all seven children have gathered around their parents' bed, all laughing wistfully together.

It may seem so ordinary, but we can underestimate the value of bedtime routines and stock phrases, the "take cares," "drive safelys" and "good luck with the math test" expressions — until we hear tragic stories such as that told by the mother of a murder victim in the film *Dead Man Walking*. The last time she saw her daughter alive, she was so concerned about the pin fixing her daughter's hem, she forgot to tell her she loved her.

Perhaps one way to gauge our family prayer and ritual is to ask ourselves what we want our children to remember after they have left our homes and begun their own. It probably won't be our words, but our attitudes, our unexamined habits, our actions so well established we no longer even think about them. Sue Bender recounts the story "Gregor's Tablecloth" as proof of the staying power of ritual. During World War II, a boy, his brother, and mother moved constantly around Europe from place to place: from hotel to inn to a friend's home and back to a hotel again. Each time they arrived in a new place, his mother would open the small suitcase filled with their belongings and bring out the lace tablecloth that she had used for the Friday night meal in their home in Poland, before they were forced to leave and begin their exile.

"At each place the ritual was exactly the same. She would place the suitcase on a table, carefully drape the tablecloth over the suitcase, light a candle, and in that moment, the place, wherever it was, became HOME."[59]

The poet Archibald MacLeish writes of his wife:

> Wherever she is there is sun
> and time and a sweet air:
> Peace is there,
> Work done.
>
> There are always curtains and flowers
> And candles and baked bread
> And a cloth spread
> And a clean house.[60]

The clean house may give some parents guilt trips, but if that is not our strong suit, then we may ask ourselves how *else* will our children remember their time in our homes? If we say we love God, we trust God, we serve God, how do our children know? Do our words and actions spring from these beliefs?

Perhaps we need to rethink ritual, including under this umbrella our ordinary daily repetitions: watering the plants, packing the lunches, brushing the hair, bathing the body, washing the clothes. The list of numbly repeated tasks can quickly turn to drudgery, unless we look at these actions through a different lens, the perspective of ritual.

Maria Harris cites theologian Kathryn Allen Rabuzzi, who sees "home" work as having a merit of its own, beyond mere production. "Rituals are actions performed with regular rhythms. A woman or a man engaging regularly in the rhythmic patterns of homemaking finds that she or he shapes the rhythm of those actions and is, in turn, shaped by them, an outcome common to most rituals."[61]

To broaden the notion of prayer as we have enlarged that of ritual, we must remember that God created over eight hundred thousand species of insects and more than six hundred varieties of the eucalyptus tree alone. Surely there are as many kinds of prayer styles as there are infinite varieties of people. What makes one child or parent gag is profoundly moving or healing for another.

Surely a sampling could include the ABC prayer for young children. Praising God in all things, they name the creations that begin with a different letter every day. On B Day, preschoolers raise a chorus of praise for "bubbles, Band-Aids, and cute bottoms." On T Day, it's "tacos, trucks, tarantulas!"

Many parents punctuate the day with "arrow prayers" — straight shots to the heart of God. They may come as the thermometer in a child's mouth tips 104 degrees, the clock ticks an hour past curfew, or the gas gauge nears empty. One mom referred to her ongoing conversation with God as "pickle jar prayer." "If the lid on the pickle jar was stuck and you couldn't get it open, would you ask your husband to do it?" she asked.

"Sure," her friend replied. "If he were there, and he could do it, he wouldn't mind."

"So? Isn't God there? Does God mind? Is there anything you couldn't talk to God about?"

Just as women and men of the monastic tradition organized their days according to the hours of the divine office, so parents may discover its rhythms in our lives. Instead of following canonical texts, we find prayer woven into the events at hand in daily life. Ours might sound like this:

Matins: "Please help me find the book report before the car pool honks!"

Vespers: "Thank God for nap time"

And I am convinced that no monk ever rose in the middle of the night with a more heart-felt prayer of thanks than the parent who hears the key finally turn in the lock at 4:00 a.m. on prom night. "Thank God we survived another prom!"

– 19 –

PAUSING TO TOOT THE HORN

B ECAUSE OF THE VERY CONSTANCY of parenting — the laundry that never ends, the baths that need repeating, the arms in and out of jacket sleeves, the cooking and cleaning, the help with school projects — certain pauses should be mandated. While some might name them ritual, it seems less formal to call them pauses to toot the horn. Parents should provide a generous allotment for children, too, considering how often we nag our kids, how rarely we praise them.

In the Irish idiom, tooting one's horn meant boasting of one's achievements. It was not as arrogant as it may first sound, but carried a subtle recognition that no one else really knows what affirmation we need. So, if we're at all practical, we bestow it on ourselves. Quickly and efficiently, we take care of the need, then move on — probably back to the laundry. The practice could, like anything else, be carried to extremes, and there were probably over-tooters and under-tooters. But, in general, it's not a bad idea for stressed parents to stop for moment to appreciate what they're about. Besides, who else has year-round access to those little plastic horns everyone else sees only on New Year's Eve?

For those who may feel that such nonsense is frivolous, it is possible to elevate the concept with a scriptural precedent. Two models image this process for us: Samuel and the woman who anointed Jesus. The former carried, interestingly enough, a horn full of oil to anoint David king of the Israelites. The latter broke open a whole jar of pure nard, an outrageously expensive perfume, to anoint Jesus before his passion.

The first story is set in a family context. Disappointed in the leadership of King Saul, the Lord sends the prophet Samuel to Jesse in Bethlehem. Samuel is impressed by Jesse's seven sons because they are tall and handsome, but the Lord cautions him not to judge by appearances. Instead, Samuel is told to send for David, the son who is tending the sheep. "Now he was ruddy, and had beautiful eyes, and was handsome. The Lord said, 'Rise and anoint him; for this is the one.' Then Samuel took the horn of oil and anointed him in

116

the presence of his brothers; and the spirit of the Lord came mightily upon David from that day forward" (1 Sam. 16:12–13).

What connection do the biblical figures have with us? The message here for parents is that the appearance can be deceptive; "the Lord looks on the heart" (1 Sam. 16:7). So much parenting effort goes into maintaining the appearance: the path cleared through the house, the hair washed, the nails trimmed, the cut bandaged, the pants hemmed, the jelly blob wiped off the homework. Simply attending to the surfaces could keep anyone busy all day, but the Bible passage nudges us deeper. How many of us ever pause to consider that we are securing that most precious of creatures, the immortal human being? Every time we rub on the baby lotion, rinse the shampoo, or soap the hands, we are anointing one in whom God delights.

Throughout the history of the Israelites, children were treasured, and barrenness was a humiliating desolation. When the prophet Isaiah describes the glory of the people, he does not mean monetary wealth or precious metals. When he wants to recall the people to themselves, to their most precious richness, he writes,

> Raise your eyes and look about;
> they all gather and come to you.
> Your sons come from afar,
> and your daughters in the arms of their nurses. (60:4)

If we have that radiant attitude toward our children, they will know. We may not need to tell them they are called, chosen, and anointed, but if we consider them precious, their bearing will show it. People with low self-esteem may have a huddled slouch. On the other hand, a woman who knows she is loved has a queenly carriage.

From infancy on, children have remarkably sensitive receptors. They can tell from the way they are diapered, carried, and touched if they are regarded as a dear treasure or another burden. That could scare us — any honest parent has had moments of despair over the expenses children incur or the large piles of dirty socks they accumulate. Because those pressures are so real, it's all the more reason for the pause to appreciate. How often do we look in delight at a boy's hair gleaming in the sun, or a daughter's sturdy arm as she serves a volleyball? Do we truly treasure the rare moments of grace? The name David means "beloved"; in some sense, every child is David and every parent Samuel.

A similar anointing occurs in the New Testament. While the four gospels have slightly different accounts, a few features are common.

The woman who poured oil over Jesus' head stood in a long line of prophets who anointed leaders as Samuel did David. She ignored the grumbling of the men, who failed to understand that Jesus was about to undergo intense suffering. Before him lay torment, brutality, ugliness, and pain. She brought him beauty, fragrance, balm, and care, as if somehow she could offset the horror ahead. How he must have relaxed beneath the soothing motion of her palms!

Her action was dismissed as a female whim and criticized as a waste of money that could have been spent on the poor. Yet Jesus defended her against her critics: "She has performed a good service for me.... Wherever the good news is proclaimed in the whole world, what she has done will be told in remembrance of her" (Mark 14:6, 9).

What is the link between this woman whom John identifies as Mary, the sister of Martha and Lazarus, and parents today? Maybe we too must courageously buck the current trend that sets our children on an unrelenting path to fame and fortune. "Wait," we must say. They don't need to learn to read at three, or attend an all-day academic preschool at four. Maybe, now and then, we all need to stay home in our pajamas until noon. Perhaps kids don't need the pressure of competitive sports at age ten. Maybe they'd rather toss around the softball in the back yard or read a good mystery. Instead of spending the last ten minutes before bed cramming for an "A" on the spelling test, maybe they'd prefer a calming back rub?

The woman gave Jesus a gift, a pause in his inexorable march to Jerusalem and death. We do not know what paths our children may take, or how much suffering waits along the way. We do know that for a few times during a few years, we have the chance to give them what she gave Jesus: beauty, relaxation, caressing care. We can tune out the critics (both external and internal) who scold us for wasting time. Now is our anointed hour; now our chance to play. Most schools teach fairly competently the skills kids need to get through life. It's our job to give them the music, color, and poetry that make the life worthwhile. Both Samuel and the prophetic woman interrupted the well-oiled routine — with oil of another kind. So we can subvert the twentieth-century pressures of "march-to-success, get-those-preschoolers-ready-for-Stanford." We can pause to anoint and appreciate.

Sometimes the pause comes in formal ritual which, if we are fortunate, captures the awe and wonder of a particular time in a child's life. This lucky juncture happened when our oldest son David was a senior in high school. Before students began their senior service projects, they were ritually anointed. As it did for King David, the ceremony marked a transition for them, from being those who are cared for, to those who care. In the chaos of life with teenagers, the liturgy created a marker, a pause for reflection. The rite gathered our hopes for our children, our prayers for their strength and our blessings on their work.

Some might question the wisdom of exposing sensitive young people to the enormity of human suffering and injustice. Perhaps it was the awareness of the seriousness of their task that prompted us to pray for them, that they might bring the touch of Christ to a hungry and hurting world.

As she watched her son being anointed, one mom, a veteran of three boys, whispered with tears in her eyes, "They may not appreciate this anointing now, but they will draw on its power when the rough times come. Maybe not now, maybe not this week, or even during this project, but eventually they will come to a realization of how much they need the Spirit. And then, this grace will be theirs."

So we blessed their hands, eyes, and ears, calling them to be "Christ's message to the world, to see with his eyes, hear with his ears, speak his words of comfort and encouragement, build his kingdom on earth." Once I had examined those tiny fingers and toes with the awe any mother feels for her first-born. Now, I realized, he was being birthed again: boy into man, adolescent into committed Christian.

Of course it's a large order for a seventeen-year-old. Perhaps that's why we called on the powers of light and drew on the force of community prayer as we blessed them: "Go forth into the world in peace; be of good courage; hold fast to that which is good; rejoice in the power of the Holy Spirit." So Samuel prayed for David, his forehead wet beneath the horn; so Mary prayed for Jesus, the oil running down his face. So can we anoint and strengthen all our children.

— 20 —

FEASTS FOR FAMILIES

MANY GUIDEBOOKS tell us how to integrate the search for God with the calendar year. They show ways to celebrate various feasts: how to make an Advent wreath or an Easter candle, how to plan a party for Mardi Gras, how to make a May basket — all wonderful ways to lighten the year's passage with the spiritual dimension.

However, it is rarer to find an interpretation of the year's feasts through the lens (slightly scratched and smeared) of family experience. Most writers seem isolated in academia, and many are celibate, developing their cool, reasoned abstractions in hushed libraries. Their readings of the gospel seem distant from the passion and heat, sanitized of the reeking Jerusalem streets where the action first took place. In these texts, we miss the interruptions, the roosters, the little kids playing in the dust, the cooking odors, the random insults tossed across the marketplace.

Jesus did much of his teaching in the midst of crowds: sweaty, noisy, jostling to hear him. No one dressed up, deposited their children in a nursery, or entered a hushed sanctuary to hear his sermon. He probably competed with the folks selling fish, the barking dogs and fruit vendors. How ironic that the same message is now proclaimed to a silent audience in their best clothes, who speak only on cue, shush their children, and try not to scratch their uncomfortable Sunday suits.

To correct that irony, we can place the essential Christian truths back in the hustle-bustle of family life where they belong. The kerygma is simplicity itself: Christ lived among us, Christ suffered and died, Christ rose from the dead. We then assert boldly that Christ continues to live this mystery through us. We can fully understand the dynamic of his life only if we continue it in ours.

The reflections that follow are probably not the stuff of kitchen table discussion, unless parents are creative about personalizing the ideas for their own children. However, if parents are serious about considering these truths, their children will benefit. The rhythms of our year can follow the lines of Jesus' life, giving each season depth.

Our efforts to enter into Christ's life cannot but be rewarded by deeper compassion, increased gentleness, more centered serenity.

Christ Lives among Us

Advent and Christmas are a good time to prompt the question, where do we birth Christ or nurture his life? Advent has been called a pregnant season, and perhaps all people can learn from it what mothers learn from pregnancy. Both seasons disrupt our comfortable clichés. During pregnancy, we surrender the identity and the control we once took for granted. Glancing into a mirror during the eighth month, I've been startled: could that blimp be *me?*

Women who are accustomed to taking charge of their lives and their decisions have those reins lifted from their hands during times of conception. The most carefully calibrated temperature charts fail. The most unpredictable, one-in-a-million chances succeed.

During pregnancy, one can do little to ensure the health or influence the development of the infant. Those who beam Vivaldi to the womb and read sonnets to the fetus seem to have forgotten that God creates the child. While we can try to stay healthy and rested, no mother ever gets up in the morning and says, "Today I'll work on the liver. Tomorrow, the ears."

Similarly, we can never predict how or when God comes. Indeed God seems to delight in surprises: Who else would have chosen a stable in a moth-eaten outpost of the Roman Empire? When we are expecting a child, we must adjust to God's unpredictable schedule and scenario. For a sense of control, we substitute an intense sense of life, a conviction of God's presence. For once in our lives, we are content to *be,* not always to *do.*

Expectant mothers may feel as vulnerable as an eggshell. We reexamine every decision in light of the child: is it safe to skate? to run a race? We learn to trust, a quality that has become almost foreign to women who work hard for their paychecks, their figures, their careers. For a time at least, we substitute a long, inefficient wait for our usual, visible accomplishments. Advent is all about waiting, which seems strange to people who live at jet-set speeds and eat microwaved meals.

At least we wait in beauty. Advent is full of sense appeal: the smell of evergreen, the taste of cookies and special breads, the sight of the creche, the texture of ribbons, and the sound of carols.

A little girl, afraid of the night, once called to her mother that she couldn't sleep. "Ask God to be with you!" called back a drowsy mom. "But I want a God with skin!" wailed the child. The reward of Advent waiting is a God clothed in human skin.

Perhaps this coming of God as a baby can be best appreciated by new parents. Every loss fades in the light of this gain, this gift, this precious and irreplaceable child. The whole nine months seems relatively short; the painful labor suddenly seems brief.

Dazed new parents are in good company. The powerful leaders of government and church were conspicuously absent from the cluster around the Bethlehem crib. Instead, the Christ child's welcoming committee consisted of ordinary folks, woozy and bewildered, dimly aware that their drudgery had been shattered and their lives had been immeasurably graced.

When Jesus chose to live in the context of a human family like ours, his choice forever blessed us. God came in something small, like a baby; something humble, like swaddling; something unnoticed, like a stable. Jesus' infancy underscores the power of the powerless, the tower of the tiny. His advent made every home a dwelling for holiness.

Christmas helps us appreciate the birthings that go into each day: the family leaving every morning, starting projects like a garden, an art class, or guitar lessons. The labor poured into every meal and mortgage payment mirrors the effort of Mary and Joseph to nurture and shelter the child. God entrusted the divine Son into the hands of two people who were probably young and confused at the time, just as God places into our hands the fragile and vulnerable newborn. In our bumbling ways, we then rise to the occasion, protect and nourish the child in our care, try to repay that initial act of trust, even flee to Egypt if that becomes necessary. So we light the candles, decorate the tree, hang holly on the porch, and create aromatic reminders that where we are, God is pleased to be.

Christ Suffers and Dies

During Lent and Holy Week we ask: Where does Christ die in us? We discover that this is no unemotional, distant Savior, removed from the stuff of our lives. Instead, he endures with us the disappointments, the tragic accidents and deaths, the draining illnesses, our failures to appreciate all we've been given, our squandered potential, the fraying of relationships, bitter arguments, betrayals, economic hardships.

All the long litany that grieves parents continues the passion of Christ. We may not recognize an affinity to him as we endure the pain of friends boasting about their perfect children while ours develop values radically different from ours or become mired in destructive relationships. Surely Christ suffers with us in more dramatic situations, too, as parents await the outcome of their HIV tests or pace the waiting room during a child's surgery.

One father reflects on his eleven-year-old son's twenty-two operations. "I ask God to guide the surgeon, the anesthesiologists, and nurses. But the hardest part comes when Nick asks, 'How many more surgeries?' I know if there's only a 1 percent chance of a complication occurring, Nick will have it. I can get angry and scream, but I can't turn from God. Who else is out there?"

Before we too lightly dismiss the pain of children, we must remember that Christ suffers in them too. When children record their fears, they are often touching and poignant: "God, help me to do my homework and not get hit." "Help my daddy to quit drinking from that bottle." A pervasive fear in children is that of abandonment, and it seems from the appalling statistics of child neglect, their fear is well founded.

Perhaps one way through Lent is to focus on a different symbol, easily accessible to parents and children, for each of its six weeks.

1. Turning

Children and parents both know the gratification of someone turning when we call that person's name. For that moment, the person's attention indicates that our interruption is more important than their particular task. A turning can be soft as ash, the traditional Lenten symbol, or gentle as snowflake. While we often think of Lent as a time when we turn more deliberately toward God, Joel suggests that the turn can occur on God's side too: "Who knows? [God] may turn and have pity and leave behind a blessing" (2:14). Counting blessings may be a better Lenten practice than relinquishing television or candy. Surely it enables us to see the light tracings God leaves in our days, the dim but unmistakable signs of divine presence.

2. Laundry

Week after week, the spin cycle allows us a few fallow minutes which — who knows? — might turn to meditation. The thump of clothes in the dryer on the sight of them flapping on the clothesline brings to mind the whole lumpy family community: all our under-wear jostled together. Children know the thrill of seeing a favorite shirt, which looked hopelessly stained, emerge from the wash look-ing clean again. "It's not ruined after all!" we chortle, impressed by the power of a little detergent.

The psalmist probably didn't imagine the modern Maytag when praying: "Cleanse me of guilt; free me from my sins.... Until I am clean, bathe me with hyssop; wash me until I am whiter than snow. ...Create in me a clean heart O God" (Ps. 51:2, 7, 10). Hebrew laundry was probably more like the process I watched, amazed, in Central America: mothers beating the clothes against rocks in the stream, so their children would emerge from their hovels in gleaming white school uniforms. Released from such an energetic wash, one could easily feel, "Let these bones you have crushed dance for joy" (Ps. 51:8).

Children and adults both know what it is to emerge from a gr-uel-ing doctor or dentist appointment. The world looks as fresh as after a rain; we return to normalcy with renewed zest. A clean bill of health can be as refreshing as clean clothes. All this, God tells us, symbolizes what it means to forgive and repent.

3. Caterpillar

The image of the caterpillar, dear to children, comes from a poem by Michael Moynahan, S.J.:

> Ever emerging God
> you are part and parcel
> of that unpretentious
> paschal process
> as we inch our way
> in caterpillic crawl
> toward your glory:
> becoming fully human.[62]

Sometimes we live in suspense, keenly aware of our incompleteness. In our typically American way, we want to "fix" things, a notori-ously unworkable approach with children. They remind us that life may be inconvenient, but that each day is gift. Much as we long to be better parents, daughters or sons, we know we miss the mark. Yet when we look back over our lives, we can see a long record of God's grace leading and molding us. How could the present be any different?

We may get frustrated when God doesn't seem to respond to our immediate expectation. "God's time" is surely one of the hardest concepts to explain to children. We are all childlike when we want it all and we want it *right now*. Yet this impatient self is the person God loves; this place is presumably where God wants us to be. The newly greening spring ground we inch along is holy.

4. Sparrows

Sparrows have biblical connotations of the little ones for whom God cares. This shouldn't come as news to parents. We've been known to drop everything in a tightly scheduled work day to attend the third-grade play. A few CEOs walk out of important meetings simply to catch a grandchild's field day. When we spend much of our energy on details and never seem to accomplish any major goal, we can console ourselves: God spends times on the little ones too.

5. Feet

Sometimes it's overwhelming to concentrate on the whole body of Christ. All the needs, the complexity, the numbers of needy people can send us running in the opposite direction. But when Jesus washed feet at the Last Supper, he gave us a model. Concentrate on one step at a time: the next step, not the next mile; the foot in front of you, not the whole body. What needs the water, the wash, the kiss of your compassion? That's enough for now.

In many churches on Holy Thursday, the feet of the people are washed in a ritual commemorating Jesus' washing the feet of his disciples at the Last Supper. As parents and children participate, they are reenacting in a public way what they do in their homes routinely: care for each other, caress, cleanse.

The similarity between the scenes struck me at a ski lodge where a group of teenagers gathered after a day of skiing. The temperatures had been particularly frigid that day, and one girl moaned in pain as she removed her ski boots. Clearly, she had come unprepared: her thin socks had offered little of the protection she needed. Her toes had lost feeling and looked white, a dangerous sign of frostbite. As my son massaged her feet and warmed them with his breath, his young face was lined with concern.

When the color and feeling gradually returned, the girl's relief was audible. Sometimes, I thought, care is like Braille, a matter not for words, but for touch, not mouthed by lips, but stroked on feet.

6. *Splinter*

Blessedly, thankfully, most parents do not often hear the child's terminal diagnosis at Children's Hospital; most children do not care for parents in wheelchairs. Yet these extreme examples alert us to the suffering of Christ under more ordinary conditions. In our homes, Christ falls, thirsts, weeps, is betrayed and consoled. Among his friends, a few stayed faithful; most did not. We live it all out again: not only the brutal crucifixions, but the smaller hurts and wrongs.

As Jesus asks the unanswerable question, "My God, my God why have you abandoned me?" many families could echo it. The widow, the unemployed dad, the alcoholic who detests herself, the parent of the drug-addicted child: they could all hurl the same question into the darkness. Can we recognize his presence in our suffering? During Lent we ask what splinters do we add to the cross of Christ?

Christ Rises in Us

Sometimes it almost seems easier to handle Holy Week than to accept Easter. While Jesus had a hard time convincing his disciples he must suffer and die, he had a much harder time persuading them he had risen. On this feast, God explodes our mindless drudgery, our unthinking resignation to "that's the way it is." We'd rather hibernate, but God stuns us with surprises. The long faithfulness *is* rewarded; those who take the Lord at his word are overjoyed when his promise is fulfilled.

Where does Christ rise in a family? The answer is easy when we think of our celebrations: reunions of several generations, holidays and trips together, joyous events like weddings and graduations. But Christ easters in us daily, in ordinary ways: a child learning to read, a sickness ended, a feud resolved. When we are too depressed or too close to personal crisis to see clearly, do we remember resurrection? Can we interpret our tragedies in the light of Easter?

One year at Easter, my aunt lay dying; in another city, a new niece was being born. Death and life bumped against each other; only the paschal mystery of Christ died, Christ risen, Christ coming again and again could help me make sense of the paradox.

Sometimes it helps parents and children to take the roles of people in the resurrection story. As a mother, I identify especially with Mary Magdalene meeting the gardener. I can understand her illogical logic:

"If you tell me where you put him, I will do the impossible. I'll carry the heavy, lifeless body alone, because I love him."

How often love for children drives parents to impossible deeds! We read in the newspapers about parents lifting cars off their children's bodies, accomplishing in a burst of adrenaline what seemed humanly impossible. But in less dramatic ways, we rise at uncivilized hours, we summon energy for our children when we are too exhausted to muster it for anyone else; we make financial sacrifices so they can have security, medical care, and education.

And sometimes they reciprocate. One August, we had taken the younger children to the lake resort where the family had gone annually for fifteen years. I was resigned to the fact that our two older children were moving into independent lives and because of multiple commitments could no longer participate in this vacation. Returning to the log cabin, I remembered how happy we had been there. At one time, toddlers spilled onto the lawn, cribs filled the bedrooms, and our older son and daughter learned to paddle a canoe. So I thought somewhat wistfully, "That chapter is closed now."

I tried to make my peace with this new stage in our family life and resigned myself to a quiet holiday. But Easter came in August when, the next day, my oldest son walked onto the porch and said, "Hi, Mom." He had rearranged some commitments and driven for four hours to be there. For the trip, his sister had lent him her new red car, which no one else in the family was allowed to touch. We captured some of the elation of the women at the tomb when we all circled David, jabbering about how he'd planned this surprise, how long he could stay, and how much it meant to have him there.

Christ Will Come Again

At one parish celebration of Pentecost, concluding the fifty-day Easter season, the homilist was somewhat sloppy in his diction. Consequently, our whole pew heard him describe an "upper room full of beer." Both teenaged sons sat up and paid attention: this was something they could relate to! What a disappointment to find out the preacher had actually said "fear."

On a more fortunate Pentecost, our homilist was a mother of ten who talked about the gifts of the Spirit that had poured into a marriage of fifty years, the tensions as well as the blessings, the twenty-three grandchildren and three great-grandchildren. Few people have the chance to look back over that personal history and reflect on the Spirit's presence during the long passage of years.

We can all see an explosion of Spirit at times, but must also recognize that presence in more simple stirrings: the fragrance of clean sheets, the satisfaction of going to bed with all the homework done, lunches made, and backpacks lined up for the following morning, a dinner where we all joke around the table, the ebb and flow of friends from the family circle, promises fulfilled and skills honed, the thrill of a child making the winning goal, sharing his sandwich with the kid who forgot lunch, completing a science experiment with precision or pitching a winning baseball game. Perhaps the Spirit's flame flickers when a child awakens, soft and sleepy from a nap, hair tangled in the sunlight.

When we interpret Pentecost for a family context, we see the Spirit in our humor and our longings, in our struggles that continue despite visible success. One of theologian Elizabeth Johnson's contributions is to describe the gift of the Spirit in terms that help us appreciate this person of the Trinity active in our homes. Johnson's book *She Who Is* credits the Spirit with fertility, novelty, creativity, healing, liberation, renewal, energy, and knitting together relationships.[63] These actions are familiar on the home front where tired, discouraged people are comforted and renewed, where they wake refreshed to face a new day and inspired to tackle new challenges.

Through the mediation of human beings, the Spirit cleanses like a laundress (Isa. 4:4), assists in birth like a midwife (Ps. 22:9–10), and kneads the leaven of kindness like a baker woman (Matt. 13:33). In early Christian art, the Spirit was often portrayed as a dove, its wings spread maternally over the believer and the early church community. A Japanese mother uses the same benevolent image as she prays for her dying daughter, Sadako:

> O flock of heavenly cranes
> Cover my child with your wings.[64]

The gift of the Spirit is symbolized sacramentally by anointing and laying on of hands: How often do we stroke oil or lotion on our spouse and our children in love? How many times do we touch: rubbing the sore shoulders at the end of the day, brushing the hair in the morning, buttoning, zipping, straightening a collar, tying a bow? One brush of the hand can convey the empathy of "sorry you sprained your ankle." We rarely see these ordinary gestures in that light, but when we are tired of parenting, or irritable, or wondering why we ever got into it, we can turn to this Spirit who creates our family community and draws us into God.

Johnson explains that the Spirit who brooded over the waters in Genesis is there at the end of the Bible, too. The Book of Revelation describes an "incredibly tender gesture most often observed in the interaction of a mother with her child or lovers with each other, [when] she will wipe away every tear from their eyes."[65] The Spirit who inspired us to launch this voyage continues to bring direction to our hope, comfort for our suffering, and the fire of love to our lives.

— *21* —

SAINTS IN ALL SIZES

IT IS HELPFUL to remember that others have also launched small boats into this vast sea of God. Courageous people throughout history have been intrigued by and drawn into this exploration of the mysterious holy one. If the way looks dim or the waves choppy, we can rely on others who have charted this course before us. They are models because they have made Christ's life the template for theirs.

Most people drawn to a particular religion or profession are attracted by a person who lives out its ideals. Abstractions lack the influence of a vital human who represents what that particular life choice is all about. For example, we major in music because Dad filled the house with piano concertos; we pursue a career in medicine because a favorite aunt shared her passion for the subject.

This basic principle also applies to those called heroes in the faith, those who are paragons of holiness. Addressing the 1996 Los Angeles Religious Education Congress, Richard Rohr underscored one difference between our contemporary culture and a sacred culture. The latter holds up its heroes, saying, *"They* are worth imitating." The Franciscans in California, for instance, named their missions (which eventually became cities) for the saints: Santa Barbara, San Jose, Los Angeles, San Francisco, San Diego. On the other hand, our young people look up to popular figures like Michael Jackson, Sylvester Stallone, and Madonna, who have little to teach the soul. The danger with deifying rock stars and athletes is that our images subtly define us. We internalize what we admire.

Vincent Harding underscores the importance of giving our children healthy role models:

> Whenever we narrate the stories of spiritually powerful men and women who have lived among us, we step up to a beautiful calling, a humanizing gift, a truly parental vocation. For in exploring the lives of heroes and heroines we are able to introduce our young to the specialness of their own lives and to the great possibilities for triumph and tragedy that are stored within them.[66]

Mary Gordon echoes the importance to young girls of looking up to heroic women who defined themselves not in terms of men but of each other. Historically, women have governed nations, founded religious orders, counseled popes, defied male authority, and often mastered some awesome tricks. Esther, Hannah, Deborah, Miriam, Rahab, Judith, Mary, Elizabeth, Anna, Martha, Mary Magdalene, Joanna, Salome, Lydia, Dorcas — the litany of biblical women can go on, contradicting any nonsense that the only way girls can count is to be "cute" or snag male attention.[67]

How, then, do parents encourage saintly, heroic role models? Our own appreciation, voiced loudly and often, introduces children to these giants. The chapter on ritual mentions celebrating the feast days of the saints children were named for or other saints important to them. Careful scouting can turn up good children's lives of the saints. One caution: some older books portray the saints as pious statues whom no child would ever want to imitate. If we present saints who are as plastic as a Barbie doll, they have little bearing on real life, and canonization means the kiss of death.

How much better to introduce our children to *human* heroes with genuine flaws as well as stellar virtues. Take St. Vincent de Paul, for instance. When his father came to visit him at the seminary, the young Vincent hid in embarrassment at his dad's muddy farmer boots. This snub despite the fact that his father was financing his tuition!

Another example of a human hero is St. Elizabeth Ann Seton, who excelled at self-deprecating humor. Her humorous view of herself is especially refreshing compared to the egotistical boasting we hear from many "heroes" in sports and entertainment today. She called herself "a poor old bit of broken furniture, good only to frighten the crows away." After she had single-handedly raised her five children and her husband's brothers and sisters, endured the deaths of two young daughters, and laid the extensive foundation for the American Catholic school system, she pooh-poohed the achievements: "A poor ruined carcass, bundled up in old shawls and flannels, I never do the least work of any kind."

The word characterizes the martyrs of El Salvador, six Jesuits and two women killed by a death squad on November 16, 1989. Amando López, for instance, liked Captain Black tobacco and somehow managed to grow African violets in a dark cloud of smoke. Ignacio Martín-Baró had studied at the University of Chicago, joked about the White Sox, and played English songs on his guitar. Joaquín López y López used to relax after a grueling weekend with an "outrageously stupid" Kung Fu movie.

We who worry about the climate of violence in which our children grow up can understand how hard the Jesuits worked to make their college, the University of Central America, a force for peace and a voice for the oppressed. Even as the Salvadoran government tried to hide its atrocities against the poor, their newspaper publicized them. "When the violence increases," wrote Ignacio Ellacuría, "we must think harder." Indeed, they brought their scholarly disciplines, research and analysis to bear on solving the gravest social problems of their time.

It is not unusual for teenagers to criticize the hypocrisy of the church, calling its wealth an insult to the homeless and starving. To such critiques, the Jesuits of El Salvador offer a healthy antidote. Young people who wonder if anyone pays the price for high ideals could for an answer count the hundred bullet holes in the Jesuit residence.

Not only the ordained clergy participated in this drama. Elba Ramos, the priests' cook, had stayed on the college campus that night in November to make sure her husband working in the gate house got his supper, and because she thought it might be a safer haven for her daughter Celina. A typical mother, she worried about her beautiful sixteen-year-old's dating. A woman of large generosity and humor, she was found with her leg flung across Celina's body, as if in a final, futile gesture to protect her.

Our children should be told how in the yard where the martyrs died, Elba's husband and Celina's father planted six red rose bushes for the Jesuits, two yellow ones for the women. On ground that had been wet with blood, new life now flowers. Just as Mary Magdalene once met Jesus in a garden and discovered that he had conquered death, so the garden remains a symbol of resurrection.

Among the uncanonized saints, Dorothy Day's story has a special appeal for parents and children. She came to God not from desperate need, but from the joy prompted by her daughter's birth. For many years Day had rejoiced in the beauties of creation: azaleas and dogwood, gulls and lobsters, driftwood fires and sea spray off her island home. Tamar's birth crowned that delight. Many parents could echo Day's description: "No human creature could receive or contain so vast a flood of love and joy as I often felt after the birth of my child. With this came the need to worship, to adore."[68]

Parents can relate not only to the beginning of Day's story; we can also see maternal instincts at work in her later life. She protested war as "the continuing passion of Christ," even as most of the country was jumping on the military bandwagon. But her opposition to war stemmed from what later pacifists have recognized as the inherent contradiction between the nurture of the vulnerable and the violence that crushes life. All the work of birthing, sheltering, teaching, tending, and feeding the young is threatened by the deliberate, organized deaths incurred by military action.[69]

Through the Catholic Worker movement she founded with Peter Maurin, Dorothy Day sought to make a world in which it is easier for people to be good. When a social worker asked her how long people could stay at these homes for the poor and marginalized, she replied, "Forever. They live with us, they die with us, and we give them a Christian burial.... They become members of the family." While her guests were often mentally ill or difficult, Day emphasized serving them with joy that carried a cost: "It is not easy always to be joyful, to keep in mind the duty of delight."[70]

With the same humor that characterized Elizabeth Seton, Day turned from the label "saint": "Don't call me a saint. I don't want to be dismissed so easily."[71]

How important that our children hear the story of Dorothy's daughter Tamar, and how Dorothy Day's love for one child grew into an "extended family" that now stretches across the U.S. Her houses of hospitality, begun in 1933 and continuing today, are honored as the "conscience of the church."[72]

The story of Martin Luther King Jr. is also encouraging to children because it began with small, human steps. That can be meant literally: the young Martin had a passion for dancing which he could enjoy only on the sly. When his father was pastor of Ebenezer Baptist Church in the forties, a dancing preacher's son would not have been smiled upon!

As an adult, King saw the children of Birmingham, Alabama, among other places, caged and demeaned by racism. Segregation laws controlled where they could eat, play, and go to school. King acted because he saw children suffocated, demeaned, and stripped of their dignity; he could not allow it to continue. He intervened not with bombs and guns, but with "organizing skill and immense faith and courage."[73] King and his followers empowered the children and their families to face dogs, water cannons, and jail. When the nation saw the televised footage of the Birmingham police force attacking its young people, it was a turning point for the civil rights movement.

King's life, like any canonized saint's, had its share of bad decisions, personal struggles, depressions, failures, and betrayals. Yet our children should know that his assassination killed not only a leader of an outstanding nonviolent movement for justice, but also the father of four young children. The oldest was only ten at the time of King's death, "devastated not only by the loss of his father, but by the notion that a man who tried to love so many could be brutally assassinated for no apparent reason."[74]

If children hear too many stories of adult models, they will naturally conclude that heroism is an adult realm which they can only grow into eventually, not join immediately. They also need to hear of courageous children such as Ruby Bridges, who at the age of six lived out much of what King stood for. The first African-American to integrate Frantz Elementary School, she attended classes for almost a year by herself because of a boycott called by white parents.

Each day, federal marshalls accompanied Ruby through a hateful corridor of hecklers who hurled abuse, spit on her, and shouted racial obscenities. It would be safe to assume that running this gauntlet would necessitate hours of counseling with a skilled psychologist. Unassisted, Ruby maintained her cheerfulness, slept well at night, and smiled compassionately on her tormenters.

Intrigued, Dr. Robert Coles set out to research what made Ruby tick. He records his findings for adults in *The Moral Life of Children* and in a children's version, *The Story of Ruby Bridges*. On every developmental chart known at the time, Ruby would have registered low, the daughter of illiterate sharecroppers, who was just learning to read herself. Yet she had a hidden strength: the support of a vibrant black community, a small church that recognized her call to a special moment in history. The minister urged them to pray for their enemies; she did. Looking back on the successful integration from the ripe old age of nine, Ruby commented, "We inched a little closer to God, and because we did, we became a little better ourselves!"[75]

A modern-day Ruby lives on. During the 1990s, when integration began in the schools of South Africa, many parents followed in the footsteps of their U.S. counterparts during the 1960s. They declared a state of siege and resisted the inevitable blending of races and cultures. Yet their children weren't so defensive. According to a report of the Associated Press, Rusel Wildeboer, an eight-year-old white girl, showed black children to their classrooms and commented, "I want to help them because they're new. I would like to have them in my class because I like them."

Through all the tales of heroes, we seek to instill in our children, "You are more than a pampered darling; you can be a saint." In contemporary culture, little Brandi or Malcolm can whine for almost anything and get it. (I will confess immediately to being a sucker for all but the oddest requests from my children.) Not to diminish the blessings of the twentieth century — we've all been grateful for penicillin and indoor plumbing. No one is criticizing the superb educations, medical care, and recreational opportunities available to our children. Yet we must at the same time instill gratitude for these blessings and an awareness that in many parts of the world parents would give their right arms to secure the clean water, central heating, or literacy rates our children take for granted. Furthermore, we must call our children to heroism. The gospel saying "much will be asked of those to whom much has been given" can be overdone and lead to guilt. We must balance the high expectation against the wonder of God's grace. But it seems almost obscene to wallow in our pleasures without a corresponding sense of service.

Visiting the Kennedy Library in Boston with my two oldest children, I was struck by an interview with one of the first Peace Corps volunteers. "Why did you join?" asked the interviewer. "I'd never done anything political, patriotic, or unselfish because nobody ever asked me to," she answered. "Kennedy asked."

(The sequel to the story is more humorous. As one of those early volunteers myself, I remember lying in a tent with monsoon rains beating down on us in Central America. A damp colleague asked the rhetorical question of the stormy tropical skies: "Any more bright ideas, President Kennedy?")

How ironic that fifteen years later, this sixties idealist should be converted by her kids. I remember when the time approached for David's confirmation, and I naively pointed out that adult membership in any community meant contributing to it.

"Right, Mom!" he agreed before unsheathing the dagger. "What do *you* contribute to our church?"

I bumbled around for an answer less abstract than a monthly check, but his question provoked an embarrassed silence. Why couldn't he be like other adolescents and raise delicate issues like sex? A friendly discussion about AIDS was beginning to look easier than this chat that spiraled inevitably toward commitment.

It wasn't long before we'd signed on for the Sunday Lunch Bunch, a parish program that provided sack lunches for homeless people downtown. As mountains of groceries loomed on the kitchen table, I realized that fixing four lunches a day hadn't prepared me to pack eighty. When we got halfway through, we discovered we'd done all the sandwiches wrong, and would have to unstick and redo them.

Then I noticed our two-year-old, with markers and slips of paper, making her contribution to the bags. She'd often seen me slip notes in her siblings' lunches — "Thanks for your help last night" or

"Good luck in the Spelling Bee!" She assumed these lunches deserved the same. But eighty notes were a formidable task for a toddler. So those who weren't smearing mayonnaise or slicing ham started writing lunch notes. The four-year-old's were wobbly pictures of trucks and battleships; the twelve-year-old sent unicorns, smiley faces, and "Have a nice day!" I hope the street people weren't insulted as they unwrapped their sandwich and found a note as well. But I trusted kids to communicate care with a surer tone and a deeper sincerity than most adults could muster.

With the same openness, children from a local elementary school recently took a huge collection of new underwear to the local homeless shelter. The children had sponsored "Undie Monday," because, as one third grader explained, "It's bad enough to be homeless. But then to have old, saggy underwear too? Yuck!"

We can praise and support our children's service and read them accounts of heroic children when they are published in the newspaper. While their stories may not appear as frequently as those of murder and mayhem, we can still find the boy who, despite his own poor health, collected blankets and raised money for the victims of a natural disaster. Girl Scout and Boy Scout troops often get publicity for their efforts to tutor younger children or give toys to homeless children.

The saintly actions we see daily are less dramatic and thus harder to recognize. But our praise for our children's actions which speak of compassion or courage, creativity or integrity, teaches them how deeply we respect their unique forms of holiness. Sanctity wears many faces and does a wide variety of deeds. But the saints all seem willing to let God shine through them, like sunlight through water drops. They seem more impressed by God's beauty and power than by anything they have contributed. Shortly before she was killed by the military, a Guatemalan peasant explained her efforts for justice: "What good is life, unless you give it away? — unless you can give it for a better world, even if you never see that world but have only carried your grain of sand to the building site."[76]

"Why bother?" Our children may ask. They are bombarded by images of a culture dedicated to the quick fix, the easy way out, the self-centered pleasure. Every advertisement beams at them a subtle yet contradictory message: "You deserve a break. Relax! Take it easy. Spend. Enjoy." The options offered children for their free time are essentially couch potato functions: television, computer, video games. Why should they hoist themselves from the easy chair to hit practice balls for their younger brother obsessed with baseball? Or lug another load of trash to the dumpster for a mom who's too tired to make the trek?

Perhaps because, as our Scripture and tradition say over and over, they are called to greatness. They were born for sainthood. In the novel *Carry Me like Water* by Benjamin Saenz, a character named Jake has every reason to be angry or apathetic. Sexually abused as a child, he now carries the AIDS virus; he is tired. But he becomes reconciled when he sees the skinny children of Juarez trying to sell trinkets to the cars coming across the borders into the U.S. His empathy for the poor, dirty six-year-olds is a new response for him. "Perhaps the death he carried within him was making him soft, but now, he didn't mind the softness. He didn't want to be hard anymore — it was too much work, a kind of work that he could no longer continue because, like the items the children sold, it was not worthy of him."[77]

If our children see themselves as the precious sons and daughters of the most high king, then the authentic, moral life becomes not a matter of bending rules and cutting corners, but a celebration of their birthright. They were created to be happy, holy, whole: anything less than sanctity is beneath them.

— 22 —

GOD OF SACRED STORY

WE EXPERIENCE GOD in the saints, in our relationships, in mountains and sea, in silence and prayer, in surprising circumstances. And we enter into God's heart through story.

The Judeo-Christian collection of tales contains some doozies. To children the stories are novel, fresh, tingling with excitement. As writer Eudora Welty explains, "Listening children know stories are there. When their elders sit and begin, children are just waiting and hoping for one to come out, like a mouse from its hole."[78] Children are no dummies. Their radar is set for the interesting stuff.

Our sacred stories can satisfy their hunger — and ours. Think, for instance, of David on his rooftop drooling over Bathsheba as she emerged from her bath. Or Lazarus, lurching from the tomb, layered in grave cloths like an onion in papery skins. Or the child's loaves and fishes that multiplied and multiplied, till more than five thousand bellies were full.

The high holy days begin with a question from the youngest child. "Why is this night different from all other nights?" he or she asks, and the answer tunnels down the ages. It comes in story, sculpted over the Easter Vigil bonfire to tell our origin and exodus. With each step we take into story, the story enters us.

One benefit of the recent renaissance in Scripture study has been the realization that the same text can be read validly through different lenses. The feminine interpretation, the literary criticism, the view from the third world — each perspective can put a different spin on a familiar passage. For instance, people living under oppressive governments, in dire poverty, teach us how to be participants in, rather than spectators of, scriptural stories.

Nicaraguan peasants know exactly what it means to be arrested at night for no reason, as Jesus was. A catechist once told Salvadoran women: "Mary's child was tortured — like your children. Mary's child was innocent — like your children. Mary's child was killed — like your children."

"No!" interrupted an *abuela,* or grandmother. "It's different. She got her child back."

Being a parent *does* make a difference in the way we read the Scriptures. Indeed, parenting, with its twenty-four-hour-a-day insistence, must color our thinking as few other experiences do. Someone may also be a waiter, a sculptor, or a student, but no occupation is as all-consuming, as close to the heart as parenting. Nor does any career continue as long. With varying levels of intensity, parenting lasts from that first stark moment in the delivery room through the rest of our lives. No matter how estranged we may feel from a particular child, the bond between us remains bone-deep, blood-fast. It affects everything we do, especially the way we approach the sacred Story, and try to interweave it with our stories.

To engage in this activity with our children invites them into mystery and calls forth their gifts of imagination and sensitivity. If they learn the process of interplay between my story and The Story, they can form a relationship with God that is more than intellectual, a unity with God that is strong as sinew.

So I began to search the Scripture. Which passages are most helpful for the frazzled parent? What lines could we keep in mind through a day that hops from car pool to grocery store to work to errands to day care center to PTA meeting to bedtime story?

If buoyancy was one criterion, brevity was another. Few parents have long stretches of quiet time in which to read a narrative sustained over five or six chapters. The days of monastic quiet have vanished, even, say my friends who are vowed religious, for them. At one point in my parenting career, I swore that if I simply slid the Bible off the shelf, some mysterious vibration cued the kids to provoke a crisis.

In the interests of fairness, I consulted friends. Knowing the broad variety of their stories, I asked: What one-liners sustain you through teething, flu, February, final exams, shots, and after-prom? As you sat with your child in the emergency room, waiting for the x-rays of the skull fracture, what phrase would you whisper for comfort? What talismans do you carry against encroaching darkness and fear? When money, energy, and time have all run out, how do you turn to God?

It turned out that "if God is for us, who is against us?" (Rom. 8:31) was a favorite. Also "the light shines in the darkness and the darkness did not overcome it" (John 1:5). And "all things work together for good for those who love God" (Rom. 8:28) sustained one mom through a harrowing financial crisis. One friend surprised me. She draws strength from a wonderful marriage; her two children are bright and attractive; her career is successful. Yet her favorite passage suggests another depth, beneath the surface her friends see. She chose "Jesus wept."

A few longer passages have helped over the long haul. The text is included here because I well remember times I couldn't find a Bible, times I was too tired to look up anything, and times that the Bible had been sent off to third grade the day I needed it.

In these words from Isaiah, God speaks:

Do not fear, for I have redeemed you;
I have called you by name, you are mine.
When you pass through the waters, I will be with you;
and through the rivers, they shall not overwhelm you;
when you walk through fire you shall not be burned;
and the flame shall not consume you.
For I am the Lord your God, the Holy One of Israel, your
    Savior.
I give Egypt as your ransom, Ethiopia and Seba in exchange for
    you.
Because you are precious in my sight, and honored, and I love
    you.
I give people in return for you, nations in exchange for your
    life.
Do not fear, for I am with you;
I will bring your offspring from the east,
and from the west I will gather you;
I will say to the north, "Give them up," and to the south,
"Do not withhold;
bring my sons from far away
and my daughters from the end of the earth." (Isa. 43:1–6)

What God tells me through this passage is, "Even if you make the wrong decisions, I'm still with you." The raging waters and fires become the snide cuts from co-workers, the disappointments in spouse and kids, the slap in the face of nasty gossip from those we once trusted. Through all this, says God, I am there.

I could never have understood such fidelity until I had children and even in a limited way began to fill that role for them. I was there when they didn't get the scholarship, didn't make the team, didn't snag the part in the play, didn't get the party invitation or date for homecoming.

In similar ways, the children have comforted me. It doesn't matter to them how much I've accomplished in a day, or failed to do — they still snuggle close. They are forgiving even when my exhaustion means their brown bag lunch won't bulge with home-made cookies. "Ahh," I've thought at such times, "so this is how accepting God is!"

God even ups the ante as if to prove the integrity of that promise. "I give nations to ransom you," and I think of beautiful places: France, Hawaii, California, with all their wealth, all wrapped with a bow and given in exchange for one undeserving creature, me. The only way it's understandable is through what I would do for my children. To bring my sons from afar and my daughters home, I would probably go any distance.

This propensity of parents to do almost anything for their kids was brought home to me by a recent newspaper story. The *Denver Post* reported that for the Thunder Ridge Elementary School production of "Peter Pan," seven children *flew*. Their flight was made possible by more than fairy dust. A flight crew of parents came backstage expecting buttons and a control panel. Instead, they were handed bull ropes.

"At every performance, one parent, Paul Woodbury, had to climb six feet up a backstage ladder and stretch to grab the rope at tip-toe level. He would then jump off, rope in tow, in order to get Peter Pan soaring through the set's window for the show's first big entrance." The accompanying photo shows his daughter Rachel flying gracefully through the nursery window. She and the other children, visibly shaking at first, caught the hang of flying after two days, learning to arch their backs, shift their weight and land gracefully as doves. I do not know Mr. Woodbury or his daughter, but I thank them for giving me the perfect image for this passage from Isaiah: if the parent will go to such lengths so that the child can fly, what more will God do for precious children?

I was startled to encounter the passage again in a totally different context. In the film *Dead Man Walking*, based on the life experience of Sister Helen Prejean, the nun played by Susan Sarandon accompanies a convicted killer to his execution. The circumstances could not be more horrible: the criminal is caged in this brutal environment because he has committed a violent murder. When Sister Helen tries to assure the murderer that he too is a son of God, he answers in surprise, "I've been called son of a lot of things, but never 'son of God.'" One wonders if his life might have been different had he known of this identity sooner.

Sister Helen reads him this passage from Isaiah, as shackled and chained, he lurches toward the death chamber. That must be the ultimate test of trust in God. If it makes sense there, in that most awful place, it must ring true in ordinary life as well.

Any parent who's helped a wobbly toddler learn to walk can relate to this passage from Hosea:

> When Israel was a child, I loved him, and out of Egypt I called
>   my son.
> The more I called them, the more they went from me; they kept
>   sacrificing to the Baals, and offering incense to idols.
> Yet it was I who taught Ephraim to walk,
> I took them up in my arms; they did not know that I healed
>   them.
> I led them with cords of human kindness, with bands of love.
> I was to them like those who lift infants to their cheeks. I bent
>   down to them and fed them. (Hos. 11:1–4)

Sometimes to heighten the personal significance, I substitute my children's names for "Israel" and "Ephraim." To make it easier to enter into the tenderness of God's heart and see the link between my motherhood and God's, I also remember two stories.

One occurred during my daughter Colleen's first year away at college. The separation between August and October was long and anxiety-ridden: Would she be homesick? survive college work? Could I stand to be away from her that long? To telescope a grueling time, Parent Weekend finally arrived, and I flew out with great anticipation.

We met beneath a portico of the Student Union, a long porch I'll always remember because we ran the length of it to each other. She didn't care about preserving her college-student dignity before any of the curious onlookers. She yelled "Mom!" and we ran into each other's arms. She wasn't an infant any more, but still I lifted her to my cheeks, as I had when she was tiny. We handle the separations better now, but at airport gates, hotels, and dorms, the reunions still precipitate intense feelings.

Perhaps a more ordinary experience of parent and child falling into each other's arms happened on the shopping mall parking lot. My younger daughter, Katie, was excited about buying her first pair of earrings, and twirled eagerly across the pavement. Emotions in children seem to translate easily into bodily expression; in her pirouettes anyone could have read her delight. But one shoe was untied. She crashed on the pavement, ripped her jeans, and cut her knee. Bleeding and crying, she crumbled into my arms.

For a guy without kids, Richard Rohr captures such moments pretty well. "Don't bother me with the facts; this is my child!"[79] he imagines a parent would say. The amazing part is, God would say it too. So much of life seems to resemble that run across the parking lot, bumbling and tripping, but all made holy by the goal. Despite our blind spots and crazy detours, we hurdle toward a God who bends down to nourish us.

I discovered Psalm 139 after so much travel that in five consecutive nights, I'd slept in five different beds. The week was hardly conducive to the rooted security and serenity that traditionally prompts prayer. But I found a different kind of peace in the psalm:

> You search out my path and my lying down, and are acquainted
> with all my ways...
> You hem me in, behind and before, and lay your hand upon
> me...
> Where can I go from your spirit?
> Or where can I flee from your presence?
> If I ascend to heaven, you are there;
> if I make my bed in Sheol, you are here.
> If I take the wings of the morning and settle at the farthest
> limits of the sea,
> even there your hand shall lead me,
> and your right hand shall hold me fast. (Ps. 139:3, 5, 7–10)

I would like my children to carry that spirit of trust in God, that serene confidence of being held fast, no matter where they travel, no matter what difficulties they encounter. But to make it concrete, I'd tell them of a mountain hike where loose gravel made a steep descent risky. Any misstep could mean plunging hundreds of feet downward. The terrain would challenge an expert hiker, which I am not.

But I hiked behind a friend. When the going got particularly tough, he'd reach back for my hand. At every turn, he'd act as a sturdy brace preventing my fall. There on a rocky slope, the psalm took on life: "You hem me in, behind and before, and lay your hand upon me."

The trust I learned there would be trivialized by words. But I hope that it has given me a sense of confidence that's contagious. From that firm base, I can encourage my children to take risks, meet people unlike themselves, enter unfamiliar territory and tackle tough projects because a hand reaches out to guide them. The path seems less steep when a friend goes along, and the path is easier when the friend is Christ.

His words must come as welcome balm to parents: "Come to me, all you that are weary and are carrying heavy burdens, and I will give you rest. Take my yoke upon you, and learn from me; for I am

gentle and humble in heart and you will find rest for your souls."
(Matt. 11:28–29) He seemed to know the chronic fatigue that goes
with parenting: the never-have-a-minute-alone-or-an-uninterrupted-
thought syndrome. To people exhausted because they stayed up all
night with a sick child and still got to work on time the next
morning, he doesn't offer another challenge. He promises rest.

Even better, he volunteers to share the burden. Yokes aren't
commonplace now, except perhaps in antique stores, but we have a
vague idea that they distributed a heavy load between several beasts
of burden. (Humans sometimes feel like they carry that much weight
on aching shoulders too, so the analogy is apt.) Too often, we oper-
ate as if we bear the whole load. We forget Jesus' assurance, "You
don't have to do it alone." So we try too much, pile more load into
arms already full, work when we're too tired to make sense, and
push our limits. Then we wonder why we make mistakes and hate
ourselves for failing again.

Just as Jesus changed the symbol of the cross from an instrument
of torture and death to a sign of salvation, so he turns the yoke of
drudgery into a sign of unity. Bearing our yoke with Christ connects
us with all who suffer: the hungry, the oppressed, the imprisoned, the
sick and bereaved. Though our sufferings may differ in kind or degree, we all bear Christ's yoke together. Doing so, we learn the truth
of the aphorism: "The worst burden is to have no burden at all."

Furthermore, the yoke image reminds us that we do not parent
alone. No matter how much I think I love a child, God loves him or
her more. Perhaps we will look back over the course of a lifetime and
say to God, "You were there when I needed you." Then we'll name
the people who helped us at crucial moments, the circumstances that
worked out perfectly, all the times when we probably did not recognize God in a multitude of disguises. On that day we may finally
recognize how closely the stories were interwoven: God's and ours.

— 23 —

PASSION OF PARENTS, PASSION OF CHRIST

T HERE COMES INEVITABLY THE TIME when the voyage grows stormy. Every parent and every child knows times of sadness and betrayal, illness and tragedy, the persistent ache beneath the smooth surface. At such moments, we want to jettison the whole notion of exploring God, despairing that the deity has any care for us. Whether we suffer numbly or in raging pain, we want to be left alone — don't impinge on our agony with God-talk.

Yet a God who cannot be with us in the terrible times cannot be much of a God; a relationship sustained only in sunshine doesn't have much depth. People who have not built up the habit of care on ordinary, stress-free days will not know how to act when the crunch or the crisis comes. If we are to push ahead on the exploration we have begun, we need to be able to turn to God when we have barely the strength to lift the head from the pillow. It's all well and good to rejoice with God over the ongoing co-creation of our children, but where is God in loss? The best theologies would say, God is right beside us, suffering with, guiding us through. Such a theology says that when God's child dies, God's heart is the first to break.

Perhaps the best place to look for a lens on suffering shared is in the accounts of Jesus' passion. Three cameos there portray parents and children suffering together. Indeed, reading these incidents through the particular lens of parenthood may help us understand, as if for the first time, that Jesus remains with us when our worst fears are realized or we endure events that we dread to imagine.

Simon of Cyrene

The first story, Simon of Cyrene, is recorded in Mark 15:21, Matthew 27:32, and Luke 23:26. When an incident is found in all three synoptics, its authenticity is well established. But the verse itself is tantalizingly brief. Mark tells us that Simon is the father of Alexan-

145

der and Rufus, so we know he is a parent. All three gospels concur that he was compelled to help Jesus carry the cross. He had come from the country, a bystander who happened to find himself along the route to a crucifixion. Roman soldiers seized Simon; clearly he did not volunteer for the job.

The skeleton of the story must be rounded out to see what it holds for parents. It's easy enough to imagine Simon, strolling in from the country, lured by the city's excitement. Perhaps it was payday, and he jingled coins in his pocket, surveyed the market stalls, and smelled enticing aromas. The urban din was probably novelty to a country bloke. We can also imagine his anticipation changing sharply as the Roman soldiers commandeered him into service and he staggered beneath a sudden load.

Often we are just as nonchalant about becoming parents. A myth of "cuteness" surrounds the concept, and we eagerly buy into visions of tiny baseball caps and mitts, or delicate socks with lace. Like Simon, reality doesn't hit until we feel the thunk on the shoulders, the weight of the burden. Kicking and screaming or numb from lack of sleep, we discover we've been dragged into far more than we ever anticipated.

Under ordinary circumstances, it is good to walk with someone. We step in synch; our shadows dance together on the path ahead; our arms brush now and then; our conversation is enlarged by the outdoor perspective. The discoveries we make, whether in our thoughts or in the scenery, are better because they are shared. While the word "companions" referred originally to breaking bread together, surely it must apply as well to this wonderful state of walking beside each other.

However, the picture shifts when the walk is coerced or we labor beneath a burden. Our children are sometimes pleasant companions — until we calculate the exorbitant cost of our walk together. The ordinary strains of parenthood are enough to halt us in our tracks: the enormous financial drain, the disruption of time and priorities, the almost constant substitution of what I'd like to do for what the child asks instead. In some cases, parents looking forward to retirement take on added responsibilities for their children's children, their invalid children, their children's college debts. In multiple ways, we bear Simon's load along a path we would never have taken voluntarily.

Where does it all lead? There is no further record of Simon, but his story can be played out today. We're intrigued by the possibilities: Did he write off his contact with a condemned criminal as bad luck and try to forget it? Or did he look back on his coerced service as one of his finest moments? Did he tell the story to his two sons, and is Rufus the one to whom Paul refers in Romans 16:13 as "chosen in the Lord," an ironic twist on "forced by the Romans"? Did Simon develop any feeling for Jesus, or was that impossible in the heat and uncertainty, beneath the threatening soldier's lash? Did Jesus, exhausted himself, thank Simon? We know enough about Jesus' courteous ways to know that Simon probably didn't walk away unrewarded. He is remembered in Christian tradition, but what memory did he bear himself? Did his unwilling burden ever become a grace?

A story in the Simon mode played out in the home of Michael and Mary Tovrea. The young couple talk openly about a twenty-year struggle with mental illness. She is "bipolar with psychotic affect"; he is "paranoid schizophrenic." They have learned to cope with their illnesses through monitoring stress, staying in therapy, and using medications. For them to have a child would throw a large monkey wrench into a delicate balance. To have a terminally ill child would seem like too much stress for the healthy person. So of course, in the Simon mode, that's where their story goes.

When their unborn child was diagnosed with the chromosomal disorder Trisomy-18, the medical warnings were ominous. Such children have only a 1 in 5,000 chance of being born alive; only 10 percent live beyond the first year. The little girl would be brain dead and Mary would risk her life carrying her. Medical bills would soar.

The Tovreas filled albums with ultrasound pictures — for all they knew, the only pictures they would have of their daughter. Mary spent most of her pregnancy in bed, making colorful baby clothes. When the baby was born, "absolutely beautiful," they bucked medical authorities and whisked her out of the hospital. "If we left her in that environment, she would surely die," says Mary quietly, with a will of iron. As feisty as her mother, Bernadette lived nineteen months, with astonished doctors telling the parents that only their love was keeping her alive.

Bernadette died with her hand in her mother's shirt pocket. Had the Tovreas been asked to sign on initially, would they have agreed? Or did they, like Simon, discover the road by walking it? Their peace is mingled with sadness, but Mary says of her daughter: "I could stare at her for hours and be completely content. She was the most beautiful sight on earth. Bernadette was my joy."

Simon continues to raise questions in our lives. When we carry the load of spoiled toddlers and ungrateful teenagers, can we see in it the cross of Christ? If our children are sick, cruel, or forgetful, do we feel the sting of Christ's thorny crown? Do we ever wrongfully place our burdens on our children? Our misguided ambitions and misplaced angers can weigh down their slight shoulders. On the other hand, admitting legitimate needs and asking our children to share them can call forth their compassion. Can our identification with Simon be transformative, so that we recognize even painful trudging as a walk alongside Jesus? Does his Calvary give meaning to the painful places in our lives?

Veronica

Catholic piety holds that Veronica wiped the face of Jesus, and an imprint of his face was left on her veil. A recent excavation contains an inscription that dates to the year 130: "to the brave woman who defied the Roman soldiers and comforted the Lord." While some may question the credibility of that story, Scripture does record Jesus' encounter with several women on his way to Calvary. In Luke 23:27–28, the women of Jerusalem weep for him. Mark and Matthew name the women who stayed until the end: Mary, Mary Magdalene, Mary the mother of James and Joseph, Salome (Mark 15:40; Matt. 27:56). (Note that the women outnumbered the men — John alone — four to one!)

It comes as no surprise that they were mothers; Jesus counsels them not to weep for him, but for themselves and for their children. Their intervention in the procession contrasts with Simon because their comfort was not coerced. They wept naturally and freely; still, they caused the sad parade to stop. To stem the tide of violence or interfere in any way with the well-oiled procedures of the Roman soldiers must have required courage. They knew they could not halt the inevitable end; the execution would continue as surely and efficiently as the cattle cars rolled into Auschwitz. But for at least a moment, comfort and tenderness had their say.

No matter how stressful our routines or how deadened our relationships may seem, no matter how bitterly people suffer, there is room for the compassionate gesture. When children or parents have walled each other out, there is still a slight crack in the door. The opening that Veronica or the women created in the crowd awaits us.

How then, do parents and children wipe each other's faces? A four-year-old with leukemia once consoled her weeping mom: "Don't worry. Jesus heals me." A dad with a critically ill wife awkwardly fixed the hair of their three little daughters throughout her hospital stay. Siblings minister to each other in ways that sometimes surprise their parents. One thirteen-year-old knew her younger brother was frightened by the prospect of surgery, so she wrote a note asking his guardian angel to strengthen him. When she hung it over his hospital bed, he felt comforted and protected. In the arena of daily life, where serious illness is not (thankfully) a frequent visitor, parents still reach out: to the child who's failed a test, to the child who's ill or in trouble, to the child who cannot kick a drug habit. And children extend their care: offering their dollars to the family finances, forgiving the angry parent, quieting down when the parent's headache throbs. What matters is not that we find the perfect words of comfort, but that we try so hard.

Esperanza, the young heroine of Sandra Cisneros's novel *The House on Mango St.*, has her own poignant struggles with poverty. But she never turns her anger on her parents, seeing them sympathetically: "My papa...wakes up tired in the dark," and "Mama's hair smells like bread."[80]

I was puzzled one Sunday morning when my sixteen-year-old son Sean wasn't in bed as usual after a late Saturday night. I assumed he'd probably gone with friends to the mall, or to the basketball court with his brother. When Sean returned, I was humbled by his story. He had not only been to church (unprompted), but had taken an elderly neighbor to breakfast afterward. All her relatives had died recently; I can only imagine how a lonely lady must have felt eating pancakes with her escort, a sophomore in high school.

I shouldn't have been startled. At age four, Sean was disappointed that we'd missed the church's Sunday collection. It turned out that he'd saved his change all week, "so the Ethiopians won't be hungry." She may take on different guises, but still Veronica extends her veil; still the women weep in compassion.

Jesus Meets His Mother

From the parent's point of view, it's the most heartbreaking scene in the passion. Catholics name it the fourth station of the cross; Scripture records Mary staying with her son until the end. What must it have been like for her to see him treated as a condemned criminal? How must she have felt, she who had cradled the infant, seeing the nail marks on skin she had stroked, the bloody welts on limbs she had loved? I have hesitated to touch my children when they are sunburned, afraid of worsening the sting. Did she want to reach out to him, yet at the same time hold back? She was there to encourage him; did he also worry that she might be ashamed?

This was not the first time Jesus had met with a distraught parent. Jairus begged him to cure his only daughter, with such intensity that the dignified synagogue official fell at Jesus' feet (Luke 8:41). The Canaanite woman made herself a nuisance, on behalf of her daughter (Matt. 15:22–28). A man whose son shook with convulsions begged Jesus to cure his only child (Luke 9:38–43). Jesus stopped the funeral procession when the widow of Nain's son lay dead upon the bier (Luke 7:11–17). In each instance, and in several others, Jesus cured the child. Now he has become the dying child, the agonized mother is his own, and he can do nothing.

That image holds immense consolation for us at times when we question everything we've done; when we know we've failed; when we can do nothing to prevent our children from suffering, when we hit the dead end, the brick wall. It is the most helpless of feelings when we who have tried to protect children from infancy must stand by, impotent. All our efforts, our skills, our degrees, our accomplishments and awards mean nothing. Stripped of our most reliable supports, we fall into silence, naked and vulnerable. Only then can we enter into the passion of Christ, the terrible, chosen powerlessness of God.

The scene holds many associations for parents. How often have we had to open our arms, letting go of our children as Mary did? How often have we lent our support or our presence to those who suffer? How often have we been filled with gratitude to the people who've been there when we felt crucified? They may not have had the right words or even the perfect motives; what counted most was, they were there. I remember seeing such faithfulness when I awakened groggily from a tonsillectomy. Beside my bed in an uncomfortable hospital folding chair sat my husband, sound asleep, but still holding my hand.

My vigils in hospital waiting rooms have been relatively few and fortunately not critical. But sitting through a child's surgery has given me a wedge to empathize with parents enduring circumstances that are more dangerous or fatal. Even years later, it is poignant to remember the hush of intensive care, the professionals poised on tiptoe, the machines humming, the conversations subdued. Days in hospitals drag too long; the slightest kindness of a nurse or friend unleashes the tears held tight. Nerves stretch taut because the stakes are high: God's dearest gifts, our most precious loves.

Little can divert people in these antiseptic halls; we long only for the day we can leave the harsh school of this hospital. Here love wears a grave face; here in grim sterility, parents and children learn to cherish each other again.

When children are born, few parents think of the Pietà as an image that will dominate everything they do. Yet in a way, it shadows our exploration because it could well mark the end: the dead parent, held by the child, or the child, limp in the parent's arms. Maribeth tells of holding her dying mother's hand while "everybody around her bed was telling her to go, you deserve it. I was the last one, and I said, 'Go home, Mom.' And she left."[81]

The saints have not been immune from such sadness. When Elizabeth Ann Seton's young daughter Annina died, the loss desolated her "as no death before ever had, as no death after ever would." Several years later, her lively fourteen-year-old, Rebecca, died of the same disease. Seton kissed the lifeless child, stroked her hair, repeated, "My Rebecca, my darling." Nineteenth-century biographies try to cloak the tragedy with flummery about angels. Seton writes starkly, "I have lost the little friend of my heart."

While some may see it as morbid, there is a profound and touching beauty in the Pietà. Both mother and child have given all in love: Who could ask more or do more? And Jesus, who bled once and who wept, continues to suffer this passion in us. The scene is repeated as parents of gang members mourn children lost to violence, parents and children in war zones grieve for each other, AIDS claims both parents and children as its victims. We cannot fathom the agony of the parent whose child has been gunned down by a crazed killer or whose day care center exploded in a random bombing. But we have a glimpse: again Mary meets Christ on Calvary. In our suffering we find solidarity with theirs and know that the heart of God stretches huge with compassion. A father once said of his daughter, "Seeing her is like having my heart outside my body." God feels that way about each of us.

Such scenes sadden but do not depress because they show us what it means to live in Christ. His dying action was to entrust his mother into the hands of the beloved disciple (John 19:25–27), and in a sense, we are all the beloved disciple. At the Annunciation the power of the Holy Spirit had overshadowed Mary. Now, with arms pinioned and hands numb, God leans toward her again. If we ever doubt that God is inclined toward us, we can remember this scene: in his last words, Jesus asks us to take care of each other. Did he consciously fulfill the words of the prophet Isaiah?

— 24 —

SNAPSHOTS ON THE VOYAGE

T HE POPE, the president, and the parent all have twenty-four-hour-a-day jobs, and for parents, little seems steady but laundry and bills. Any glimpses we get of joy come in short frames, like snapshots. Unlike the Kodak families of the ads, real families seem inevitably to miss the Moment. A cute scene with the kids is a sure guarantee that the camera is lost or the flash fails. Even when everything seems to work, we get the developed pictures and stare puzzled at the backs of heads or fuzzy, distant faces. "Who are these people, and why did we take their pictures?"

The mental pictures may be more reliable than photos, and we can collect these over a lifetime. A daughter in a swimsuit whizzing down a water slide captures the essence of summer; a grin glows over the birthday candles; a child's familiar face pokes out of a Halloween costume; a thermometer drops into the beautiful normal range.

The images in these mental albums can carry us back through a child's whole life, pausing for favorite moments in the story. The evocative smell of baby oil brings back memories of infancy: the doll-sized sleepers with feet, the nightly snuggle with a little one who makes sleepy, unintelligible sounds, the pure delights of silken skin, no chin, and a wobbly head. During this time, we are filled with awe that, flawed and unsure as we are, we have played some part in the creation of this wondrous new person. All is possibility. The limitations, disappointments, and tragedies that may lie ahead are obscure; we simply enjoy sweet sensuality and beckoning potential.

Toddlerhood with all its challenges is still a unique launching into independence. With tummies leading, preschoolers charge off down new paths and climb mysterious peaks — even if these are all located in the back yard. The first words are charming; parents rush to record these gems in the baby book. New dangers hover; we also rush to baby proof the house. With endless energy, these whirling dervishes discover the wonders of stairs, insects, drapery cords, and breakables. Beneath our exhaustion runs admiration: the infant who had been totally dependent is now taking those first, absolutely necessary steps beyond us.

Elementary school represents another flowering. As our children learn to read, calculate, spell, write, analyze, and organize, we stand in awe of their skills — and the teachers who draw them forth. Humor sparks our conversations like a welcome newcomer as we hear complex analyses of the baseball team or the third-grade social mores. Parents who may have felt isolated before can now enjoy the camaraderie of others in the same boat.

High school is described elsewhere in this book, but these last four years at home have a special poignancy. The fleeting time is punctuated by milestones: driver's license, first job, homecoming, games, plays, concerts, parades, college application and acceptance, prom and graduation. Beneath all the activity, the parent may wonder, "Have I told him everything I wanted to? Have I given her all I can?" I remember a holy nun reflecting, "What an accomplishment it must be to stand before God and say, 'I have secured a child.'"

"No," I argued. "The accomplishment is saying, 'I have launched a child.'"

Now that my older daughter, Colleen, is in college, I look back on pictures of her as an almost bald baby, thin because she has suffered two bouts with pneumonia in her first year of life. Huge, dark eyes well in a pale face. She wears a pink smocked dress and a matching bonnet, feeble attempts to lend her some color.

If we ever measure miracles, this will be high on the scale: she is now a beautiful young woman with a shining mantle of dark hair. Articulate and compassionate, she has worked as hard on social issues as on maintaining her presidential scholarship. By what unfathomable grace do I deserve to call her daughter? I was the klutz of my class; she plays soccer with aplomb and dances with grace. I didn't have the courage to speak publicly until I was in my thirties; she addresses large public gatherings without butterflies.

Like frosting a cake, she tells me regularly that I have played some part in this drama, that much of her maturation is due to my role model. I am flattered, but also know when I'm in over my head. Some graces are beyond us; this is clearly one. Words cannot touch this gratitude; sometimes aging eyes well with tears of appreciation.

During pregnancy, most parents pray for a child who is healthy; we get children who, in myriad ways, are extraordinarily gifted. (By this I do not mean "gifted" as in IQ scores or programs for the musically talented. We all know the Down's syndrome child with an exceptional capacity for love, a child with a physical challenge and a great gift for art, a Special Olympics winner whose smile lights the skies.)

And we are not the first to plumb this mystery. Presumably Mary did diapers; one can safely guess that she wondered where the wisdom, the miracles, the deep compassion of her adult son originated. Was it she who gave Luke the line, "the child grew and became strong, filled with wisdom; and the favor of God was upon him" (2:40)?

Where is God in our snapshot collection? It's a daily tribute to God's faithful presence in our homes that children grow bigger without our even noticing, take on adult skills while we are still paying their bills and claiming them as dependents on our taxes. "When did all that happen?" we ask in surprise at the official markers of passing time: birthdays, award banquets, bar mitzvahs or confirmations, graduations, weddings. During days that seemed ordinary, when we were intent on finding the homework and getting to school on time, these caterpillars in our midst were, with minimal fanfare, turning into butterflies.

If we have participated in the process with one child, we are more prepared for its surprises in another. While the first one who appears unconcerned about lousy grades may bring on the parental stomach ache, we gradually gain perspective on later crises. Sure, it's tough not to have any friends in the fourth grade, but we also know that can change the following year. The mean teacher seems like an ogre who will ruin the little psyche and may give us some sleepless nights, but we also learn how her influence can be mitigated by time.

As we have seen, each stage has its unique graces, and our time together is short. While it is in the nature of joy itself to be fleeting, even snapshot memories leave us a lasting legacy. Sister Wendy Beckett writes: "Joy establishes us so securely in itself, and in the remembrance of its presence, that we can cope with whatever life has to throw at us."[82]

Such a gift came on a rainy Saturday morning, when only Katie and I were home. We both knew without saying a word that the weekend was special, because it was bracketed on both sides by trips that would take me away from her. Neither of us was really traumatized by the prospect of our time apart. The trips were brief and Katie looked forward to the activities with her siblings and the day camps we'd planned for the week ahead. So I do not know what drove us to it, but we did something we had not done since she was much smaller.

Without a word of introduction, we climbed into the rocking chair together and rocked, with no sound but the rain around us and the thunk of the wood on the floor. It was infinitely comforting. We did not speak, so I do not know where her fantasies took her during that half hour. But I was carried back to times when she was one or two or three, a tiny body that fit easily into my arms. Now she was eleven, and she still fit; there was simply a surplus of legs hanging over the arms of the chair.

Where did we go as we rocked? Perhaps into some still quiet place where we were one despite trips and age and growth and all the thousand things that transpire to pull parents and children apart. Perhaps we'd found some psychic island where her contours still conform to mine, and my heartbeat pulses in her ears. After a while we returned to our tasks, but we resumed the routine with a touch more peacefulness, I think. People who write about prayer talk about being centered and secured; the effects of this time were much the same. And who's to say a rocking chair can't be sacred space, or rain a hymn, or a mother and child together some echo of another madonna?

— 25 —

FULL CIRCLE

IT'S TOUGH TO SEE a pattern when we're enmeshed in anything, but parenting seems an especially murky forest in which to identify the trees. That makes it even more precious when we sense the completion of a full circle.

The circular pattern can take many forms, as several examples show. A homilist once told the story of Bill Havens, who trained hard to represent the United States at the first canoeing event in the 1924 Olympics. But Bill faced a dilemma: his first child was due to be born the day of the race. Bill's wife encouraged him to go, but he decided to stay with her instead. The team won; Bill missed his chance for a medal; the baby was three weeks overdue.

Twenty-eight years later, Bill's son Frank phoned him from Helsinki. Frank had taken up canoeing, too, and he was calling to tell his dad that he had won for him the Olympic medal which Bill had passed up long ago.

Bill was fortunate enough to see fruition in his lifetime, but many parents know first-hand the truth of the saying, "No seed ever sees the flower." The seeds we plant in our children may flower long after our limited life spans. For example, in Mildred Taylor's novel *Roll of Thunder, Hear My Cry*, an African-American family leads a store boycott against the local merchant's continuing injustices to their community. A sympathetic white lawyer warns that the boycott may be ineffective. "Still," says the father, looking at his daughters and sons, "I want these children to know we tried, and what we can't do now, maybe one day they will."[83] To illustrate his words, we might begin drawing a curve, but leave the circle incomplete.

Sometimes the circles reaches completion beyond the immediate family. When I was asked ten years ago to sponsor a woman entering the Catholic community, I worried about the time commitment, the theological background I might lack, and the church rites that would require a shy introvert to go public. I never anticipated the riches the experience would bring.

One of whom arrived on the scene a year after the young woman joined the church: a small, blond son. Would I be his godmother?

We joked about "twofer the price of one," but it was as great an honor to hold the baby as the baptismal waters flowed over him as it had been to place my hand on his mother's shoulder as she was confirmed.

Eight years later, as the small blond boy received his first communion, I looked across a sea of heads at his mother. Between us was an understanding too rich for words: together, we had given a little boy the best we knew. The power of Eucharist that had bonded two women in friendship was now filling his life, as he spoke proudly of growing old enough to come to the table with the adults. That first communion day of springtime flowers, white suits, lace, and song marked a beginning for the children, while at the same time it gave us a sense of completion: a cord tied, a loaf firmly kneaded and braided, a circle closed.

For most parents and children, the experience of God in the ordinary is paramount. For the Haas family of Denver, God entered through the drama of catastrophic illness. When their third daughter Sarah was born, Tony was working as a church music director and Janet was busy with Hannah and Becca. Mother and baby seemed healthy and went home from the hospital. Then disaster struck: Janet became critically ill, had three serious surgeries, and spent a hundred days in the hospital. Doctors resuscitated her after her heart stopped on the operating table.

During this ordeal, the church community gathered around the family in prayer and support, providing meals, child care, housecleaning, and driving. Janet's name appeared on the prayer chains of many religious denominations; other children prayed especially hard that three little girls not lose their mom. In retrospect, Janet said, "When I gazed upon God's face, it was their faces I saw: those who helped clean our house, those who ran errands, those who held me in their prayers."

To the church that had stood so staunchly with the family, Janet returned to speak the following Mother's Day. Quiet and petite, she told her story without histrionics, but with a moving calm. While she had endured the first seven weeks of her illness in a drug-induced coma, she was in shock when the full impact of the situation hit her. Then she became angry: Why did she have to be the sick one in the family? Why must she miss out on Sarah's first few months of life? Janet said, "Besides the physical challenges like learning to walk again and caring for an open wound and ileostomy, I faced many emotional battles. I longed to have just one normal day."

Prayer was difficult, but Janet's mom assured her that her suffering was the only prayer she needed. Knowing that God could not take away her pain, Janet asked simply to lie in God's arms and feel some peace in the madness. She found the perfect analogy for her prayer one day when Sarah was crabby from teething. The baby insisted that Janet carry her everywhere she went. Janet writes, "Finally, instead of fighting her, I sat down in the rocking chair, held her close, and let her relax in my arms. I could feel her whole body go limp, and her breathing fell into the rhythm of mine." Similarly, there were many times throughout the illness when Janet let God mother her, surrendered control, and fell asleep in God's arms. It's a lovely image of interlocking circles: the baby in the mother's arms, the mother in God's.

Janet's older daughters learned to rejoice in her simple presence. Here was a puzzling mom who couldn't run and play as she had before, who could barely walk or hold the baby. But she was home, and that was all they needed. They spent hours on her bed, helping with dressings and medical supplies. They even adjusted their pace so Janet could keep up on crutches or a cane. In the process, they learned compassion for the sick and accelerated Janet's healing by assuring her, "You're almost a real mommy!"

The Haas children learned this language of care, Janet pointed out, not from their parents' preaching, but from their gentle actions. Janet and Tony place a high priority on weekly church attendance, but believe firmly that "it is how we live day to day that teaches our children about God." She quotes Acts: "Without exception, the crowds that heard Philip and saw the miracles he performed attended closely to what he had to say" (8:6). The action gets their attention; then they will attend to the words.

"You are living stones," Peter told his community (1 Pet. 2:5). We may ask ourselves what kind of stones we are. Janet concluded, "I am like a geode, because it is only when the rock is broken open that the real beauty is visible."

While the Haas family didn't really have a choice about Janet's illness, they could choose how to handle it. Other families would have fought the disease with anger and bitterness, but they found through it what a gift life is. While no one can predict their futures, one suspects that when Hannah, Becca, and Sarah face their own crises, some trace of their parents' faith-filled attitude may resurface in them.

Because travel has been a metaphor throughout this book, it is appropriate to conclude with the Haases' journey through death to new life. For those whose travels stay closer to the loop of school –

work – grocery store – home, a story told by Cardinal Newman may also provide closure.

He tells of a man who wanted all his life to visit Rome. (Today's equivalent might be Epcot, Cancun, or Disneyland.) When he finally arrived in Rome, stepped out on his balcony, and admired the view, he could not believe he was finally there. By repeating to himself and his family members, "Here I am in Rome!" he finally convinced himself of his good fortune.[84]

We too can cultivate the awareness of blessing that enabled the Haas family to focus on life in the teeth of death. Like the visitor to Rome, we can tell ourselves, "I am loved and redeemed." "I am fortunate to have the children or parents I do." "I am happily home, right where God wants me, right where I belong."

It is startling to overhear our children voice an expression which we ourselves use often — especially embarrassing when it's a curse! Their tendency to mimic could also work positively, and our gratitude could become contagious. Henri Nouwen writes a motto families could hang on the refrigerator: "When we keep claiming the light, we will find ourselves becoming more and more radiant."[85]

Parents and children do not voyage toward God in the same way that clergy, women religious, or even other families do. But as the families described here have shown, each unique step is sacred. All the processes of exploring, homecoming, finding God in surprises, guiding, storytelling, suffering, and celebrating lead to one end.

Those fortunate enough to have glimpsed the bottomless, boundless joy of God through this process of discovery look attentively for it afterward. Ernesto Cardenal draws an analogy to sea creatures who "retain the memory of the sea, even when they have been put in an aquarium, and still go on moving with the rhythm of the waves, no matter their distance from the sea."[86]

When we're tempted to avoid or abandon the quest, we can remember Bilbo Baggins, the reluctant hero of *The Hobbit*. Asked to join a perilous adventure, he dreads surrendering his cozy home, Bag End. He sums up the dilemma facing us all: "Oh, dear. I may regret this. I will *probably* regret this. But I might regret *not* going...*more*."[87]

The adventure that awaits us can be resumed again and again. When we become irritable, tired, or depressed, we can settle into the ocean of God once more, trusting ourselves to those powerful waves, then, like the sea creature, *remembering*.

NOTES

1. Augustine, *The Confessions of St. Augustine,* trans. E. B. Pusey (New York: E. P. Dutton, 1951), 151.

2. Quoted in Carol Flinders, *Enduring Grace* (San Francisco: Harper, 1993), 52.

3. Quoted in Sheila, Dennis, and Matthew Linn, *Good Goats* (New York: Paulist Press, 1994), 45.

4. Eugene La Verdiere, *Dining in the Kingdom of God* (Chicago: Liturgy Training Publications, 1994), 9–13.

5. Patricia Killen and John De Beer, *The Art of Theological Reflection* (New York: Crossroad, 1995), 51.

6. Christopher Fry, *A Sleep of Prisoners* (New York: Oxford University Press, 1951), 47–48.

7. Maria Harris, *Proclaim Jubilee!* (Louisville: Westminster/John Knox Press, 1996), 58.

8. Ibid., 59.

9. Marian Wright Edelman, *Guide My Feet* (Boston: Beacon Press, 1995), 71.

10. Barbara Kingsolver, *High Tide in Tucson* (New York: HarperCollins, 1995), 106.

11. William Jarema, *There's a Hole in My Chest* (New York: Crossroad, 1996), 7–31.

12. Anne Rowthorn, *The Liberation of the Laity* (Harrisburg, Pa.: Morehouse Publishing, 1986), 61.

13. Matthew Fox, *Meditations with Meister Eckhart* (Santa Fe: Bear & Co., 1983), 15.

14. Thornton Wilder, *The Bridge of San Luis Rey* (New York: Washington Square Press, 1969), 180.

15. Wendy Beckett, *The Gaze of Love* (San Francisco: HarperSanFrancisco, 1993), 48.

16. Peter Meinke, "Untitled," quoted in Gabriele Rico, *Writing the Natural Way* (New York: St. Martin's, 1983), 45.

17. Richard Rohr, *Radical Grace* (Cincinnati: St. Anthony Messenger Press, 1995), 61.

18. Rachel Carson, *The Sense of Wonder* (New York: Harper & Row, 1956), 42–43.

19. Terry Tempest Williams, *Refuge* (New York: Pantheon, 1991), 140.

20. Clarissa Pinkola Estes, *Women Who Run with the Wolves* (New York: Ballantine Books, 1992), 514.

21. Megan McKenna, *Lent* (Maryknoll, N.Y.: Orbis Books, 1996), 62–63.

22. Walker Percy, quoted in Robert Coles, *The Moral Life of Children* (Boston: Houghton Mifflin, 1986), 29.

23. Richard Rohr, *Radical Grace* (Cincinnati: St. Anthony Messenger Press, 1995), 390–91.

24. Matthew Fox, *Meditations with Meister Eckhart* (Santa Fe: Bear & Co. 1983), 29.

25. Terry Tempest Williams, *Refuge* (New York: Pantheon, 1991), 147.

26. Paul Philibert, "Landscaping the Religious Imagination," in Eleanor Bernstein and John Brooks-Leonard, eds., *Children in the Assembly of the Church* (Chicago: Liturgy Training Publications, 1992), 17.

27. Ibid., 23.

28. Richard Rohr, *Radical Grace* (Cincinnati: St. Anthony Messenger Press, 1995), 192.

29. Ibid., 131.

30. Mary Gordon, "Getting Here from There: A Writer's Reflections on a Religious Past," in William Zinsser, ed., *Spiritual Quests* (Boston: Houghton Mifflin, 1988), 28.

31. Ibid., 31.

32. Ibid., 34.

33. Ibid., 40.

34. James Carroll, *Wonder and Worship* (Paramus, N.J.: Newman Press, 1970), 70.

35. William Silverman, *Rabbinic Wisdom and Jewish Values* (Union of American Hebrew Congregations, 1971), 127.

36. Marian Wright Edelman. *Guide My Feet* (Boston: Beacon Press, 1995), xxi.

37. Quoted in Julia Cameron, *The Artist's Way* (New York: Putnam's, 1992), 20.

38. Ibid., 29.

39. Ibid., 2.

40. Sue Bender, *Everyday Sacred* (New York: Harper Collins, 1995), 59, 45.

41. Ibid., 44.

42. William Jarema, *There's a Hole in My Chest* (New York: Crossroad, 1996), 29–30.

43. Charles Shelton, "Reflections on the Mental Health of Jesuits," *Studies in the Spirituality of Jesuits* 23, no. 4 (September 1991): 33.

44. Archibald MacLeish, *J. B.* (Boston: Houghton Mifflin, 1958), 38.

45. Ibid., 40.

46. Ibid., 138–39.

47. Thomas Merton, *The Seven Storey Mountain* (Garden City, N.Y.: Doubleday Image Books, 1970), 17.

48. Ibid., 35.

49. May Sarton, *Collected Poems* (New York: W. W. Norton, 1993), 72.

50. Richard Rohr, *Radical Grace* (Cincinnati: St. Anthony Messenger Press, 1995), 228.

51. Maggie Pike and others, *Parent Child Retreats* (Denver: Living the Good News, 1997).

52. Marian Cowan and John Futrell, *The Spiritual Exercises of St. Ignatius of Loyola: A Handbook for Directors* (St. Louis: Le Jacq Publishing, 1982), 48.

53. Rohr, *Radical Grace,* 391.

54. Thomas Merton, quoted in M. Basil Pennington, *I Call You Friends* (St. Louis: Creative Communications for the Parish, 1996), 2.

55. Henri Nouwen, *Life of the Beloved* (New York: Crossroad, 1995), 56–57.

56. Sheila, Dennis, and Matthew Linn, *Sleeping with Bread* (Mahwah, N.J.: Paulist Press, 1995).

57. Maya Angelou, *I Know Why the Caged Bird Sings* (New York: Bantam Books, 1993), 5.

58. Victor Villasenor, *Rain of Gold* (Houston: Arte Público Press, 1991), 34, 37.

59. Bender, *Everyday Sacred,* 59.

60. Archibald MacLeish, "Poem in Prose," in Oscar Williams and Edwin Honig, eds., *The Mentor Book of Major American Poets* (New York: New American Library, 1962), 441.

61. Maria Harris, *Proclaim Jubilee!* (Louisville: Westminster/John Knox Press, 1996), 59.

62. Michael Moynahan, *Orphaned Wisdom: Meditations for Lent* (New York: Paulist Press, 1990), 48.

63. Elizabeth Johnson, *She Who Is: The Mystery of God in Feminist Theological Discourse* (New York: Crossroad, 1993), 135.

64. Eleanor Coerr, *Sadako and the Thousand Paper Cranes* (New York: Putnam's Sons, 1993), n.p.

65. Johnson, *She Who Is,* 138.

66. Vincent Harding, *Martin Luther King: The Inconvenient Hero* (Maryknoll, N.Y.: Orbis Books, 1996), 128.

67. Mary Gordon, "Getting Here from There: A Writer's Reflections on a Religious Past," in William Zinsser, ed., *Spiritual Quests* (Boston: Houghton Mifflin, 1988), 43.

68. Dorothy Day, *The Long Loneliness* (New York: Harper & Bros., 1952), 139.

69. Sara Ruddick, *Maternal Thinking: Toward a Politics of Peace* (New York: Ballantine Books, 1989), 148.

70. Day, *The Long Loneliness,* 285.

71. Cited in Jim Forest, "There Was Always Bread," *Sojourners* 5, no. 10 (December 1976): 13.

72. Joyce Hollyday, *Clothed with the Sun* (Louisville: Westminster/John Knox Press, 1994), 174.

73. Harding, *Martin Luther King,* 133.

74. Ibid., 136.

75. Robert Coles, *The Moral Life of Children* (Boston: Houghton Mifflin, 1986), 36.

76. Penny Lernoux, quoted in Hollyday, *Clothed with the Sun,* 99.

77. Benjamin Saenz, *Carry Me like Water* (New York: Hyperion, 1995), 502.

78. Eudora Welty, *One Writer's Beginnings* (New York: Warner Books, 1983), 16.

79. Richard Rohr, *Radical Grace* (Cincinnati: St. Anthony Messenger Press, 1995), 390.

80. Sandra Cisneros, *The House on Mango St.* (New York: Vintage Books, 1989), 56, 7.

81. Ed Will, "Someone You Love Has Died," *Denver Post,* July 23, 1996.

82. Wendy Beckett, *Meditations on Joy* (London: Dorling Kindersley, 1995), 21.

83. Mildred Taylor, *Roll of Thunder, Hear My Cry* (New York: Dial Press, 1976), 165.

84. John Henry Newman, "On the Difficulty of Realizing Sacred Privileges," *Parochial and Plain Sermons,* vol. 6 (London, 1924).

85. Henri Nouwen, *Life of the Beloved* (New York: Crossroad, 1995), 52.

86. Ernesto Cardenal, *Abide in Love* (Maryknoll, N.Y.: Orbis Books, 1995), 24.

87. J. R. R. Tolkien, *The Hobbit,* a Play adapted by Edward Mast (Woodstock, Ill.: Dramatic Publishing, 1996), 18.

BIBLIOGRAPHY

Angelou, Maya. *I Know Why the Caged Bird Sings*. New York: Bantam Books, 1993.

Augustine. *The Confessions of St. Augustine*. Trans. E. B. Pusey. New York, E. P. Dutton, 1951.

Beckett, Wendy. *The Gaze of Love*. San Francisco: HarperSanFrancisco, 1993.

———. *Meditations on Joy*. London: Dorling Kindersley, 1995.

Bender, Sue. *Everyday Sacred*. New York: HarperCollins, 1995.

Cameron, Julia. *The Artist's Way*. New York: Putnam's, 1992.

Cardenal, Ernesto. *Abide in Love*. Maryknoll, N.Y.: Orbis Books, 1995.

Carroll, James. *Wonder and Worship*. Paramus, N.J.: Newman Press, 1970.

Carson, Rachel. *The Sense of Wonder*. New York: Harper and Row, 1956.

Cisneros, Sandra. *The House on Mango St*. New York: Vintage Books, 1989.

Coerr, Eleanor. *Sadako and the Thousand Paper Cranes*. New York: Putnam's Sons, 1993.

Coles, Robert. *The Moral Life of Children*. Boston: Houghton Mifflin, 1986.

———. *The Spiritual Life of Children*. Boston: Houghton Mifflin, 1990.

Cowan, Marian, and John Futrell. *The Spiritual Exercises of St. Ignatius of Loyola: A Handbook for Directors*. St. Louis: Le Jacq Publishing, 1982.

Day, Dorothy. *The Long Loneliness*. New York: Harper & Bros., 1952.

Edelman, Marian Wright. *Guide My Feet*. Boston: Beacon Press, 1995.

Estes, Clarissa Pinkola. *Women Who Run with the Wolves*. New York: Ballantine Books, 1992.

Flinders, Carol. *Enduring Grace*. San Francisco: Harper, 1993.

Forest, Jim. "There Was Always Bread," *Sojourners* 5, no. 10 (December 1976).

Fox, Matthew. *Meditations with Meister Eckhart*. Santa Fe: Bear and Co., 1983.

Fry, Christopher. *A Sleep of Prisoners*. New York: Oxford University Press, 1951.

Gordon, Mary. "Getting Here from There: A Writer's Reflections on a Religious Past." In William Zinsser, ed. *Spiritual Quests*. Boston: Houghton Mifflin, 1988.

Harding, Vincent. *Martin Luther King: The Inconvenient Hero*. Maryknoll, N.Y.: Orbis Books, 1996.

Harris, Maria. *Proclaim Jubilee!* Louisville: Westminster/John Knox Press, 1996.

Henri Nouwen, *Life of the Beloved*. New York: Crossroad, 1995.

Hollyday, Joyce. *Clothed with the Sun*. Louisville: Westminster/John Knox Press, 1994.

Jarema, William. *There's a Hole in My Chest*. New York: Crossroad, 1996.

Johnson, Elizabeth. *She Who Is: The Mystery of God in Feminist Theological Discourse*. New York: Crossroad, 1993.

Killen, Patricia, and John De Beer. *The Art of Theological Reflection*. New York: Crossroad, 1995.

Kingsolver, Barbara. *High Tide in Tucson*. New York: HarperCollins, 1995.

La Verdiere, Eugene. *Dining in the Kingdom of God.* Chicago: Liturgy Training Publications, 1994.

Linn, Dennis, Sheila, and Matthew. *Good Goats.* Mahwah, N.J.: Paulist Press, 1994.

————. *Sleeping with Bread.* Mahwah, N.J.: Paulist Press, 1995.

MacLeish, Archibald. *J. B.* Boston: Houghton Mifflin, 1958.

McKenna, Megan. *Lent.* Maryknoll, N.Y.: Orbis Books, 1996.

Meinke, Peter. "Untitled." In Gabriele Rico, *Writing the Natural Way.* New York: St. Martin's, 1983.

Merton, Thomas. *The Seven Storey Mountain.* Garden City, N.Y.: Doubleday Image Books, 1970.

Moore, Thomas. *Care of the Soul.* New York: HarperCollins, 1992.

Moynahan, Michael. *Orphaned Wisdom: Meditations for Lent.* New York: Paulist Press, 1990.

Newman, John Henry. "On the Difficulty of Realizing Sacred Privileges," *Parochial and Plain Sermons.* Vol. 6. London, 1924.

Nouwen, Henri. *Life of the Beloved.* New York: Crossroad, 1995.

Pennington, M. Basil. *I Call You Friends.* St. Louis: Creative Communications for the Parish, 1996.

Philibert, Paul. "Landscaping the Religious Imagination." In Eleanor Bernstein and John Brooks-Leonard, eds. *Children in the Assembly of the Church.* Chicago: Liturgy Training Publications, 1992.

Pike, Maggie, and others. *Parent Child Retreats.* Denver: Living the Good News, 1997.

Rohr, Richard. *Radical Grace.* Cincinnati: St. Anthony Messenger Press, 1995.

Rowthorn, Anne. *The Liberation of the Laity.* Harrisburg, Pa.: Morehouse Publishing, 1986.

Ruddick, Sara. *Maternal Thinking: Toward a Politics of Peace.* New York: Ballantine Books, 1989.

Ruether, Rosemary Radford. *Women-Church: Theology and Practice of Feminist Liturgical Communities.* San Francisco: Harper & Row, 1985.

Saenz, Benjamin. *Carry Me like Water.* New York: Hyperion, 1995.

Sarton, May. *Collected Poems.* New York: W. W. Norton, 1993.

Shelton, Charles. "Reflections on the Mental Health of Jesuits," *Studies in the Spirituality of Jesuits* 23, no. 4 (September 1991).

Silverman, William. *Rabbinic Wisdom and Jewish Values.* Union of American Hebrew Congregations, 1971.

Taylor, Mildred. *Roll of Thunder, Hear My Cry.* New York: Dial Press, 1976.

Tolkien, J. R. R. *The Hobbit.* A play adapted by Edward Mast. Woodstock, Ill.: Dramatic Publishing, 1996.

Villasenor, Victor. *Rain of Gold.* Houston: Arte Público Press, 1991.

Welty, Endora. *One Writer's Beginnings.* New York: Warner Books, 1983.

Wilder, Thornton. *The Bridge of San Luis Rey.* New York: Washington Square Press, 1969.

Will, Ed. "Someone You Love Has Died," *Denver Post,* July 23, 1996.

Williams, Terry Tempest. *Refuge.* New York: Pantheon, 1991.

OF RELATED INTEREST